LESSONS IN WITCHCRAFT

About the Author

Perhaps the most widely published Wiccan author of her time, Silver RavenWolf's books appear all over the world. She has completed eighteen books for Llewellyn Worldwide, including the bestsellers *Solitary Witch* and *Teen Witch*. Artist, photographer, and Internet entrepreneur, Silver also heads the Black Forest Clan—a Wiccan organization that consists of 53 covens in 29 states and 3 international groups. Wife of 25 years and mother of four children, Silver has been interviewed by the *New York Times*, the *Wall Street Journal*, and *US News & World Report*. Visit her website at:

HTTP://WWW.SILVERRAVENWOLF.COM

SILVER RAVENWOLF

A Witch's
NOTEBOOK

LESSONS IN WITCHCRAFT

Llewellyn Publications
Saint Paul, Minnesota

Dedicated to Hugh Irving and Healers' House

FIRST EDITION
Second Printing, 2005

Book design by Rebecca Zins
Cover design by Kevin R. Brown
Interior illustrations © 2004 by Dorothy Reinhardt

Llewellyn is a registered trademark of Llewellyn Worldwide, Ltd.

Library of Congress Cataloging-in-Publication Data
RavenWolf, Silver, 1956–
    A witch's notebook : lessons in witchcraft / Silver RavenWolf. —1st ed.
      p.   cm.
    Includes bibliographical references and index.
    ISBN 0-7387-0662-0
    1. Witchcraft.   I. Title.

  BF1566.R34 2005
  133.4'3—dc22

2004063266

Llewellyn Publications
A Division of Llewellyn Worldwide, Ltd.
P.O. Box 64383, Dept. 0-7387-0662-0
St. Paul, MN 55164-0383, U.S.A.
www.llewellyn.com

Printed in the United States of America
on recycled paper

Contents

Introduction

I have notebooks lying all over the house. They are collecting dust in the attic, in boxes in the basement, shoved in my magickal cabinet, under my bed, in the kitchen drawers, teetering on top of the massive bookcase in the living room, and poking out from beneath the dining room hutch. I don't write in code, but if you perused them they would probably look like a chicken went wild with a calligraphy set. Okay, change the chicken to a raven and at least it is a more mystical visualization.

If I stacked all these notebooks together and put them in date order, I could trace my path of enlightenment—filled with interesting twists, amazing testimonials, and several flat-on-my-face accounts of life in the Witch lane. Here's one on my runic studies, one on the tarot, and several on my Pow-Wow studies. Oh! And this one! My Druid initiation and elevation . . . here's the complete set of my journey through Witchcraft (that's a thick bunch), several on modern and classical astrology, and plenty on my more recent Hoodoo studies (compliments of Llewellyn author Ray Malbrough). There's even a bunch of Reiki notes here, including my Master Attunement. Yep, it's like I've been on a magickal bus, traveling all over the place, learning neat new things, and incorporating those lessons into my everyday life.

If I put all of my notebooks together on the table I can definitely see a transition occurring. Through stories about people, about situations, events, and in the early days about how I felt deep inside (lots of that), I slowly reached out into the universe, grasping at the idea of pure potential. Episodes of the daily grind in the earlier notebooks were replaced by dissertations on life, aspects of the divine, my purpose (what was it?), reality, magick, history, symbolism, and so on. It wasn't that I'd distanced myself from day-to-day living (yeah, with four kids, a husband, numerous pets, a nine-to-five job . . . I think not). Instead, I made up my mind that there was a way to mesh spirituality, magick, science, and real life into a harmonious tapestry—and I was going to find it!

I'm still working on my enlightenment and it's been a fantastic journey. This notebook takes the best of those experiences and moments of exciting education and formats them into useful lessons focused on modern science and spirituality for the beginning and advanced student that can be studied alone or with other material. You'll find the writing a bit different in this book, as sometimes I found myself speaking to the student and sometimes to the teacher. There is an explanation for this; as of the completion of this particular work, I have fifty-three covens in the United States and Canada. My daily life within the Craft is often busy with the governing of our clan, working with our teachers, designing teaching rituals, formats, events, correspondence, and general material. We don't hive—we multiply! Given this current focus, my work has moved into the arena of teaching the teachers, not on basic study (they've already done that) but on group government that works, methods of presentation, philosophy of our religion, and the joys and stresses of imparting to students this amazing practice we call Witchcraft.

May you at least find one pearl of useful wisdom among these pages!

About This Book

Welcome, fellow passengers! The path to enlightenment—where does it start and where does it end? Well, it doesn't. Your journey began before you manifested in physical form here on this planet and it will not cease when that physical representation of yourself is no longer capable of interacting with this world. Our journey is not linear; it is a series of energy unfoldments out of space and time that represent our choices and our understanding of them. This understanding sometimes occurs before, during, or after the direction was chosen—it is never the same. Our journey is nothing more than utilized pure potential at any given observation point (notice I didn't say the word "time"). Our understanding, then, in essence, is enlightenment.

The itinerary for this tour is the book you are holding, *A Witch's Notebook*. It is a series of successful techniques that I've used over the years in an effort to understand myself, my children, my friends, religion, spirituality, the science of magick, and the world around me. It is a small representation of my personal notebooks, and therefore need not be used in a linear fashion, although if you choose to do so it will function very well as a set of lessons for the initiate. Each topic is a mini-lesson in and of itself. Above all, the work is designed to encourage you to think, to be creative, and to forge your own path (which will be different than mine). Its fundamental teachings are rooted in modern Witchcraft, but the techniques we will use cover a compendium of magickal sciences and ancient philosophy, and can be incorporated into various study programs. If you are new to Witchcraft or the occult sciences, please note that this book is designed as a hands-on work and does not cover a vast array of explanation; therefore, you may wish to read my book *Solitary Witch: The Ultimate Book of Shadows for the New Generation* (Llewellyn, 2003) for further clarification on various points of Witchcraft, including historical, researched, and annotated material, or choose a different Craft-related book to enhance your understanding. Each lesson in this book contains a primary aspect for contemplation. For example, part one focuses on the aura. From this contemplation is borne the exercises for you to try. The exercises in each part can be used by new and experienced students alike. How you choose to incorporate them into your daily practice, and in what order you choose to do so, is up to you. Many of these exercises incorporate sacred symbols from a variety of cultures. You may be familiar with these symbols or they may be new to you. Although I have given brief explanations throughout the text, I urge you to carry your studies further as you work with each symbol, visiting the library, surfing the Internet, recording your dreams, etc.

In this book I provide a step-by-step study guide that any student can use to enhance his or her spiritual training. The material can be employed alone or in tandem with other occult-related books and lessons. Each part was designed to work from moon to moon, moving the student through five months of training that will be intensified by their own life experiences along the way. Use a sixth month to review what you have learned.

In the beginning I planned to write thirteen full lessons, then dropped that number. As I worked through the material with my own students, I realized that five sections was more than enough to cover half a year's training. The other half could be spent in Craft dynamics, group work, and historical research, should the instructor feel this information applies to the training process they have chosen. My sole purpose was to combine modern science and spiritual pursuits into an easy to follow format. I hope this book serves that purpose for you.

May you be cleansed, blessed, and regenerated in the names of the Lord and the Lady. So mote it be.

ONE

Exercises in This Section

Cleansing

In most orders, when an initiate first enters the magickal environment, the art of cleansing and consecration is taught as the beginning step in the unification of body, mind, and spirit. We learn to cleanse our environment and ourselves before moving on to the more interesting aspects of training. Because it sounds boring and tedious and less-than-important ("I wanna be powerful, get healed, and become great, wonderful, spiritual, and all that good stuff, so let's skip this and get to the secret stuff"), this fundamental building block of all magickal practice, except in the most serious of groups, normally gets a slight nod, a quick flick of the broom, a slash of the smoking sage wand, and on to the "more important stuff" we go.

In most training environments, teaching the cleansing process is normally done in stages (we gather an awful lot of crud as we go along in life), incorporating a wide variety of techniques, each designed to lighten our psychological burdens and dust-bust our energy field (sometimes called the auric body) so that we can emotionally, mentally, and physically welcome the unlimited potential available to us. This potential has always been there and can be accessed by anyone—we just get bogged down, sometimes, and don't see it. Cleansing techniques allow us to rise above old, negative patterns and prepare ourselves to welcome new techniques with a compendium of shining choices to make. Too, going through the cleansing process prepares us to join the group mind (whatever that group may be). By doing proper cleansing exercises, the student's insertion into the

one

two

three

four

five

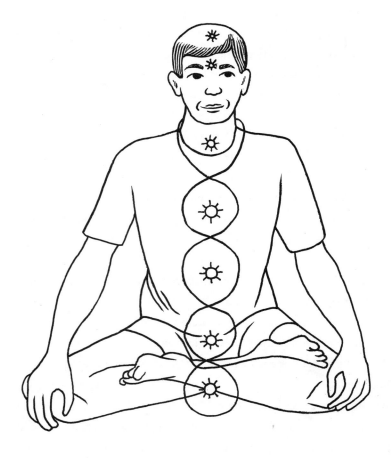

*The chakras, from top to bottom: crown, brow/third eye, throat,
heart, solar plexus, sacral, and base.*

group mind is not as disruptive—as opposed to an individual who wants to bring their baggage with them and dump it on everyone else. Anyone who has worked closely with magickal groups can tell you that a student who does not practice cleansing and consecrating techniques on a regular basis is akin to running a lawnmower with a never-ending supply of gas through your favorite flower bed.

That's fine and dandy for the new student—but what about us old-timers? Well, I hate to say it, but many of us tend to forget about the importance of these very simple techniques. We gotta pay bills, teach students, listen to drama, get the kid to soccer practice, (listen to drama), take the car in for repairs, (listen to drama), go to work and deal with Attila the Hun (deal with the drama), play crash cart at the grocery store on Friday night, and on and on. It is too easy, quite frankly, to forget about something as overtly simple and as necessary as cleansing. Yet the very first thing you should do when you step into any mental mud puddle is cleanse. Why? I thought you'd never ask!

The Aura

The standard definition of the aura goes like this: Scientists agree that every person, place, or animal has a rainbow-like energy field, called an aura, that pulses around the corporal body. In people, the aura is a measurable electromagnetic field close to your skin that can, depending upon your emotions and the state of your health, reach as far from the body as thirty feet. Between the top of your head and the base of your spine there is an electrical potential of around 400 volts, which is part of the body's electromagnetic field. The layers of your aura send messages to your brain all the time. Your aura is linked to the physical body by the seven energy vortexes of the body, called chakras (Sanskrit for "wheel of light"). Together with the life force known as chi (cosmic energy), the aura and the chakras work to maintain your overall balance and good health.

Okay, so you've read all this before (possibly). Now, let's bring quantum physics into the picture, which states that everything is made of nothing, yet morphs into something. The new theory of the atom is that particles of matter are actually chunks of energy whose pattern is formed by their sluggish state; should they be moving faster, the matter would not be there or would be something altogether different (your table would be a table one minute and a plant the next). This slow-motion behavior is akin to a "frozen" state, and the frozen state of each chunk is equated to a process. Life is filled with moving from one process to another. Matter (like the table), says this new science, is the gross representation of light patterns—which means that anything that is corporal is last on the manifestation list, the product of a very slowly moving pattern that gives us a dimensional result in this plane. If that is the case, then our "real" body is not the bones and flesh one; it is simply a pattern projection of the light body (not the other way around). If this is true, then your light body is your primary energy pattern, not the secondary resultant one. This means that the "real" healing or change of anything on earth (people, animals, plants, bugs, smelly bog creatures) must manifest first in the auric body, which will then realign the physical body—create, destroy, or repair—once the change has been put into action. Such changes are created by thought (light).

Just as the physical body is a magnet for all sorts of interesting beasties throughout the day, so, too, does your auric body collect undesirable energy patterns—the physical body, remember, is a replication of the auric one. As above, so below; just as we have gross tools to cleanse the physical body, so, too, do we have energy tools to cleanse the auric body: thought, light, and sound. These tools are interchangeable and can affect both the auric and the physical bodies.

If we shift our primary concentration from the physical body to the auric one, what will happen? If you spent the next week concentrating on auric fields rather than corporal objects, what do you think would occur? That is your first contemplation exercise for this lesson. If you are experienced at working magick, try performing various aspects of your working keeping this idea in mind.

Once you have spent time seeing the auric field as primary, then switch to perceiving the physical body and the auric body as a balanced whole. How does that change your perception? Could it be that the chakra vortexes (seven major ones and twenty-one minor ones) are the lenses through which the corporal body is actually projected?

Auric Visualization Techniques

I have three simple visualization techniques in my notebooks that have been useful to me over the years, especially in the realm of personal healing and attaining balance. Easy to perform on a daily basis, they require only one week to set the patterns firmly in your mind—from there you can practice them every day for at least thirty days (which is suggested) or use them in a way that fits your lifestyle. The more you practice, the more benefit you will receive from them. They deal, in essence, with light. Those who have used this technique have stated that it is like floating in a pool of light. One student commented, "It was like when I was a little kid learning to float on my back. I found the sensation comfortable and extremely relaxing."

Liquid Light

Sit in a quiet place where you will be undisturbed for at least five minutes. Take three deep breaths and exhale slowly. Close your eyes. Envision white light encompassing your auric body. Imagine that the light coalesces into a glittering, sacred liquid of spiritual, mental, and physical transformation. Allow this liquid light to pour into your auric field from all edges of the auric body. The path of the light slowly flows into your heart chakra from all directions until you are totally filled with pure white light energy. Continue until no speck of darkness remains and you feel your inner self vibrating with pure potential and power. Take three deep breaths and open your eyes. The exercise is completed. If you like, begin and end the session with the soft sound of a bell or chimes.

SPIRITUAL USE: This visualization assists in cleansing the auric body and opening blocked areas for the acceptance of positive spiritual change.

PRACTICAL USE: Rather than running for over-the-counter drugs when illness is lurking, if I can catch that moment when I know I'm "getting it," I will repeat this visualization right before bed until I fall asleep. In most cases I awaken without the symptoms of the previous night. However, it took me several years to listen to my body and learn that it sends subtle signals when illness is about to strike. This means that the auric field is already under attack and the physical malady is yet to follow. I'm sure you've all had that feeling where you have acknowledged your body's signal by saying "I bet I'm gonna get sick!" yet felt helpless to do anything about it. Maybe you experience a tingling sensation, light-headedness, etc., a full twenty-four hours before you actually feel any overt physical symptoms, which may be dull warnings in themselves—burning in the sinuses, a mild headache, and so on. This visualization works best the moment you realize that illness is sniffing at your auric field!

Higher Mind Attunement

Begin with the liquid light technique. Sit in a quiet place where you will be undisturbed for at least five minutes. Take three deep breaths and exhale slowly. Close your eyes. Envision white light encompassing your auric body. Imagine that the light coalesces into a glittering, sacred liquid of spiritual, mental, and physical transformation. Allow this liquid light to pour into your auric field from all edges of the auric body. The path of the light slowly flows into your heart chakra from all directions until you are totally filled with pure white light energy. Continue until no speck of darkness remains and you feel your inner self vibrating with pure potential and power. Take a deep breath and relax.

Now envision your heart chakra glowing white (there are no colors in this visualization). Next, think of your throat chakra glowing with bright, intense light, just as you did with the heart chakra. Move up to the third eye chakra, and finally to the crown chakra, lighting them up like a pinball machine. This part is easy. The next takes a little effort!

You are going to connect these chakras in a continuous spinning loop of energy. Begin with the heart chakra and visualize the energy spinning not from side to side but from top to bottom and back up again within the chakra. Once you have this mental spinning motion going, part of the energy whips up to the throat chakra, spins top to bottom and back to top several times, then moves up to the third eye chakra, repeats, and then spins up to the crown, spins, then shoots down and back to the heart. This is a visualization of loops within loops and is easy for some, difficult for others—just don't give up. Of the three techniques this may take longer to master, but it is well worth the effort.

Begin with attempting to create the loops within loops five times. Each day add a loop (if you are brave, add in a sequence of five). If you lose the visualization, gently draw your mind back to the technique at hand. When you feel completely calm and have lost the visualization yet again or have completed the desired number of repetitions, take three deep breaths and open your eyes.

SPIRITUAL USE: If the student is preparing for a coronation, initiation, a martial art, or a new form of enlightenment pattern through self-study, this exercise clears out negative blocks and strengthens the connection to the higher self. I was required to do this visualization every day for nine months before my spiritualist coronation. It was well worth the effort.

one

two

three

four

five

9

PRACTICAL USE: This is an excellent technique to use prior to the employment of any divination tool, a study session, or in a test-taking environment. Add spearmint fragrance, tea, or essential oil to any spellworking where you wish to use this particular technique for clarity of mind.

"No Mind"

This technique brings us right back into the realm of quantum physics and places us smack in the headlights of Zen Buddhism (a popular avenue for enlightenment that has coined the phraseology,[1] yet the premise of "no mind" is at the heart of just about any serious esoteric study). If you have always wondered what they're playing with at the higher levels of magick, this is it. Socialization and pageantry are *not* at the root of alchemical studies; however, the group mind does have a massive influence in the success or failure of joined workings, as many of us have noted over the years.

The place of "no mind" is where all manifestation begins. It is the void, yet—it is not. It is blank, but it is full—definitely a state that must be meditated upon for total understanding within the self. "No mind" is the process of finding perfection within the moment, and in that perfection, stillness; and in that stillness, enlightenment; and in that enlightenment, peace. It is from the place of "no mind" that perfection in what we do can be attained to the best of our capabilities.

The practice of understanding "no mind" requires that we once again change our perception of the world and our place in it.

---

1. "Zen," Microsoft Encarta Online Encyclopedia. Zen is the peculiarly Chinese way of accomplishing the Buddhist goal of seeing the world just as it is, that is, with a mind that has no grasping thoughts or feelings (Sanskrit *trishna*). This attitude is called "no mind" (Chinese *wu-hsin*), a state of consciousness wherein thoughts move without leaving any trace. Unlike other forms of Buddhism, Zen holds that such freedom of mind cannot be attained by gradual practice but must come through direct and immediate insight (Chinese *tun-wu*; Japanese *satori*).

I say "once again" because any study toward personal spirituality truly is a succession of perception adjustments made by the self. If you have been a student of the occult for many years, you may be nodding your head and at the same time marveling at the sheer number of adjustments you have made since you began your journey of enlightenment. If you are new to esoteric studies, then the excitement that perceptual changes can actually make you happier and the world a better place is an exhilarating experience. You *can* make a difference, because magick is as real as the mind—a blatant fact that everyone but the true occultist is afraid to say due to that little yet powerful beastie, the ego.

"No mind," they say, does not come from practice; it simply wakes one day from one dreamtime to another, filling us with an amazing sense of wonder that we are all one—that the tapestry of this plane and everything in it is connected one to the other. This awakening sometimes occurs in direct response to initiatory practices and other times as a result of our personal studies, choices, relationships, etc. The paths are many; the realization is one.

Yet we are human after all, and that realization does not always stay with us as we battle with the school system, deal with a techno-sweatshop job, find ourselves enmeshed in an enabling situation, rub sore feet because our employer demanded we work a double shift, are thrown back into a repetitive psychodrama that has haunted us since childhood, or discover that our grandmother is dying or that our significant other has been spending all those late nights in the arms of another. Our emotions, coupled with our ego, override our moment of grace and we again find ourselves deep in the trenches, living to fight another day in stress, hardship, worry, and sometimes despair. Too often we act out of ego (our own or the pressures of others) rather than learning the art of patience, which is just as difficult as endeavoring to study a new field of science—from scratch. It is far more difficult to teach an eager student patience than it is to take them through an entire year of classical astrology complete with William Lily's three-inch master volume of horary data! Therefore, holding on to "no mind" and continuing to live and breathe in our daily lives is far more difficult than attaining it in the first place, which is what this third exercise is all about: learning how to hold on to "no mind" long enough to raise our higher spiritual vibrations and make strides forward, rather than falling back into comfortable, familiar, negative patterns. It is from "no mind" that magick is born, and anyone can do it—if you hold the key.

The first part of this exercise can be done anywhere, at any time, and is excellent if you are under any type of stress. The theme is Perfection of the Moment. That's it. That's all there is to it. No matter what you are doing, stop. Just "be." Observe without thought. This is extremely easy to do with things that are beautiful or artistically rendered, yet it might take a few tries if your teenaged son is screaming in your face or that control-freak supervisor of yours is marching the aisles and telling you "Please put both feet on the floor" and "No, you are not allowed to have pictures of your family members in your cubicle." When we focus on anything in the moment, all emotion ceases—there is no pain of the past nor fear of the future, because the focus is "now." It is from this type of moment, honored ladies and gentlemen otherwise known as Witches, that magick is born.

So! I challenge you to practice this moment of perfection for at least a week—a month is even better. If you stick with it, I assure you that you will have amazing personal journal entries, because once you begin this exercise (and keep it up), totally mouth-dropping things can occur.

After you have practiced "perfection of the moment" for at least a week, add it to the auric exercise sequence. Begin with the liquid light technique. Sit in a quiet place where you will be undisturbed for at least five minutes. Take three deep breaths and exhale slowly. Close your eyes. Envision white light encompassing your auric body. Imagine that the light coalesces into a glittering, sacred liquid of spiritual, mental, and physical transformation. Allow this liquid light to pour into your auric field from all edges of the auric body. The path of the light slowly flows into your heart chakra from all directions until you are totally filled with pure white light energy. Continue this visualization until all areas of the field are pulsing with the white light. Now, simply experience the perfection of the moment. When you are finished, breathe deeply three times, exhaling slowly, and open your eyes.

SPIRITUAL USE: The benefits of "no mind" are enormous. Through learning and practicing this technique on a daily basis, even small things become golden and the spirit begins to shed years of uncomfortable, negative baggage. In enlightenment there is cleansing.

PRACTICAL USE: The "perfection of the moment" is the point when all empowerment of any item, place, person, or animal is accomplished. After practicing this sequence, students may find ritual, spellcasting, and meditation far easier to accomplish. Life trials (you know, the ones your students keep trying to drag into circle?) may at least diminish or, at best, become balanced—and, as a result, resolved with less than normal effort as the anticipated emotional agonizing over an issue is completely dissolved in the practice of "no mind."

Interestingly enough, there are side effects to this third technique. They may include:

- Psychic flashes during "no mind" meditations—see it, let it go.

- Moments of absolute clarity in waking life. Celebrate it.

- Increased production and creativity in daily activities. Acknowledge it.

- Difficulty sleeping. You need to detoxify, which may include cutting back or dispensing with the junk food, alcohol, cigarettes, and caffeine-related products. Adding a simple exercise program is a fine suggestion. If you feel moved in that direction, you might want to try yoga, tai chi, or a more physical martial arts program, landscape your garden or spruce up the basement, join the gym or find a drumming class near you. Physical activity allows the mind, body, and spirit to work in balance, which is why many esoteric orders require you to put in so many hours of muscle-crunching physical labor. There *is* a purpose, after all. You cannot die and take your toys with you, but you *can* bring beauty to your temporary playground.

Student Comments on the First Three Exercises

During the process of putting together the first three exercises, several Black Forest members and friends were kind enough to give me their comments. One woman who has battled several medical issues due to a horrendous car accident had this to say about the exercises, and I believe her words will be incredibly helpful to you.

> I did practice these first two sections at various times of the day, various conditions—rested, tired, in pain, "medicated," etc. Although after I had arrived at the ability to become "liquid" (a new sort of instant alpha in the liquid form for me), the effect became predictable. Relaxed, focused, more awake, more attuned, and even refreshed. Interesting.
>
> But then there was the section on the "no mind" and the perfection of the moment. *I had arrived.* Okay, this one returns us to where we know we need to be. Almost as if all those memories we had forgotten were resurfaced.
>
> When I was a child, I was sure I could see and taste the air. Of course, I was told that was impossible and forgot how to do so. I knew the patterns of the wind, I heard the grass speak. (I know, I

should have been locked up at an early age, right?) Anyway, I had forgotten all those things until this exercise.

The first time I tried the third exercise, I was still aware of all the noises in the neighborhood, and the cats cleaning their paws on my bed, and the sound of the traffic down the street.

The second time I went through all the sections getting here, and it was as if I became one with "The Force." Even in the dark, I was able to see the particles in the air, and taste them . . . I was even sure I could identify the memory of those tastes from my childhood . . . I could tell which way the air in the room was moving. The sound of the quiet had its own "instruments" playing; I could feel the difference of cool and warm areas all over my body. I could smell the earth that existed in the textiles in my room. I remember being aware that my heart had sped up, as did my breathing, but it was as if they were just more sounds that made up the moment than something I "needed." I was without need.

I was just being in the moment, witnessing things I knew but had forgotten. Like breathing out takes about twice as long as breathing in . . . how amazing is that! Or that it seemed like I could have counted the threads in the cotton sheet I was laying on, but never felt before—as if it mattered how many threads existed, and all of a sudden I could smell the sheep it was derived from . . .

I had to keep bringing myself back to "the moment," since the instant you start discovering things (even in a miniscule segment of time), you start to "think" and lose it again. I recall coming back to the moment several times after becoming amazed at where it led me, then . . . I fell asleep. Obviously, the next time would have to be in the upright position and in daylight.

Although it is now the thing I do on the way to bed, it is better than anything one could take for sleep . . . because it reminds you on the way to resting your mind and body that only the body actually rests, the mind and spirit just go someplace else while they wait for the physical to catch back up . . .

During one of my day exercises, I realized a couple of things, the least of which is that when you need to decide what is really important, go back to what you knew first. What you sense and therefore know because it was retrieved by the purest routes in

one

two

three

four

five

15

which you collect data: your senses. They have not been polluted by someone else's knowledge. And they can be retrained to return to their optimum functioning. Bringing yourself into the "here and now" gives you a whole new outlook on any moment or space of time, which really is a bigger picture in itself.

Most importantly, this exercise reminds us that all that data and energy we collect in a day, an hour, or a lifetime, although important, detaches us from a really big reality. We are all connected to everything that exists around us, even if we have become unaware of its existence. Bonding with that basic energy when we attain just existing in a perfect moment reminds even those of us who may occasionally wonder why we are walking around on this Earth/what we are here for . . . that we are here because our very existence is connected to everything else . . . and that is enough. It is bigger than anything we can accomplish in the physical form.

I had the experience of feeling like I had shrunk into "nothingness" while attempting to get there. But when I arrived, I was bigger than this package that houses my mind and spirit in this life.

Thanks for this one. It is my routine now. Even if I forget to brush my teeth, I manage for a bit each day to leave my body and the world that doesn't matter as much as the one that really exists; long enough to remind myself of what does matter.

The Good, the Bad, and the Truly Ugly

Over the years I've gotten into the practice of thinking "cleansing" first, no matter what the circumstances—whether the focus is on creating a successful career, weaving family happiness, or dealing with the compendium of life's big and little issues. From the cleansing activities performed by any student, the gifts of balance and peace of mind are integrated into daily life. Unfortunately, many of us don't take the time to enact cleansing procedures when things are perking along nicely (other than perhaps a wave of the sage), and we totally let go of the thought when the walls of our mind are covered with emotional goop because of a recent negative event. No matter what head-rip the student may bring to my attention, my first two questions have always been "Have you done any type of cleansing?" and "Have you done any magickal applications to improve your circumstances?" In many cases, even though the student may be well experienced in the art and science of magick or magico-religious practices, because they are emotionally distraught over any given problem, the answer to both questions is often first silence, and then "no." In an equal number of responses, the answer to the first has been "yes," but "no" to the second question. Only on occasion do I receive an affirmative answer to both questions. Why is this?

Emotions are wily creatures. They pull us up, they smash us down, and we may have an entire soap opera in our heads even before the situation hits the pavement outside of ourselves. Emotions are often debilitating in stressful situations—they drag us through mental mud, wring us out, and stomp on us. Add a chronic medical condition (which is sometimes the case) and you are certainly dealing with a full plate. Regardless, it is difficult, even for the most practiced of students (at times), to find the energy to deal magickally with a problem because we are so exhausted from the trauma of the emotionally charged experience. Whether it is your girlfriend leaving you, the bank bouncing twenty of your checks because of their own error and now acting likes asses when you need them to fix the problem, losing your job, dealing with the terminal illness of a family member, or finding yourself lost in a quagmire of red tape on a legal issue, remembering to cleanse and then choosing the right magick is often lost in the emotional maelstrom. Even though we may move quickly through the cleansing part, choosing what would be right in the order of magick can sometimes be as difficult as the problem itself. If this occurs, it is usually because the student did not spend enough time on their cleansing procedures to gain the emotional distance they need to tackle the problem with a clear head. In this case, the answer is to go back to cleansing if a choice seems too complicated. Indeed, from a scientific view, cleansing the aura trans-mutes the negative semi-frozen pattern (frozen because it has several observers), changes the pattern through the light process or by pulling the pattern into the void (your choice of visualization), and re-freezes the new pattern. Okay—take a moment and think about it. If this is so—that by using our thoughts directed in a peaceful, nonviolent, "no mind" way, we can literally change anything we wish, and that we simply have to acknowledge this fact to make it so—then there is nothing we cannot accomplish. I believe there were a few historical sages preaching this very same thing—stand up and be counted!

Smaller issues can be equally frustrating and just as mind-numbing, depending on all those other things going on in your life at the same time. Taking that necessary step of cleansing—every day, if necessary, until the issue ceases to be your main focus—is truly one of the best favors you can do for yourself. You don't have to make it a huge orchestrated process—there are many techniques; but do make the attempt. One small step leads to another, drawing you closer to emotional stability because you are doing something about how you feel, even if it is only lighting a candle, taking a spiritual bath, or spending a few minutes concentrating on filling yourself with white light. The more you do to help yourself, the easier it is to deal with the trauma and the closer you are to completing a full cleansing ritual, followed at some point by a chosen magickal appli-cation (or whatever your goal is). Yes, it is a wonderful thing to vent to a friend, but they cannot do the work for you—that is your re-sponsibility. If you think it is their job to help you, then you are de-ceiving yourself by your own impatience and lack of self-confi-dence. Change and the tools you need to handle this problem always begin *within* yourself, not outside of yourself. Once you acknowl-edge that you are capable of handling the issue at hand, then the real work can begin. This is an extraordinarily hard lesson for all of us to learn.

Keeping this in mind, you may wish to try any or all of the remaining exercises in this chapter.

Empowering a "No Mind" Auric Cleansing Candle

For this exercise you need only a white candle and about ten uninterrupted minutes. Soft music that fills you with a sense of peace and balance can be added for psychological effect. The size of the candle depends upon your analysis of the situation at hand. If things are going well and there are no real difficulties to speak of, a votive will do. If you are dealing with one of those little bumps in life, choose a candle that burns for at least 48 to 72 hours. If you have a massive problem, start with a nice, big, fat pillar candle.

This exercise is best done on your feet where you have room to move, however it can be adjusted (as you see fit) for those who do not have freedom of movement. Above all else, take your time with the exercise and attempt to make your movements as gentle and free-flowing as possible. If you feel a little tense before you begin, try a few neck and shoulder rolls, envisioning the stress leaving your body, followed by several deep, relaxing breaths. Depending upon your previous training and the circumstances at hand, it is at this point that you may choose to activate a circle casting.

Stand comfortably straight with your feet about twelve to fifteen inches apart. With your eyes closed, envision your auric body surrounded by white light. When this visualization is stable, open your eyes. With both hands, hold the unlit candle a little out in front of you between the heart chakra and the solar plexus. The most important factor is to keep your mind empty. Remember what "no mind" feels like (from the earlier exercises you were given) and simply enjoy the sensation of the exercise. Slowly raise the candle until it is even with the crown chakra; your head will be bent back slightly. As your eyes are on the raised candle, you will be looking heavenward. Now lower the candle in a straight line down past the third eye, throat, heart, solar plexus, down past the root chakra, and down to a bit above the ground. Slowly raise the candle back up to a point perpendicular to the heart chakra. With this bodily movement you have done two things: joined the energies of heaven and earth and made the magickal statement "as above, so below." You have also just performed a pre-alignment of the meridians of your body. In doing this, every time you work through a sequence to empower any object, you will also be benefiting in a healthy way regardless of whom the object is for. While holding the object and applying this process, you may feel your hands begin to tingle (or be hot or warm), which is a sign of energy being transferred into the object. You may also feel that life's cares are slipping away. This is very good!

The next step is to gather the energies from the four elements of this planet: air, fire, water, and earth. There has always been a debate in the magickal community on whether to move clockwise or counterclockwise during various applications of enchantment. I believe this debate has arisen partly due to our physical location— whether you are above or below the equator, and from which direction the air current normally flows where you live. In this exercise, because I live above the equator, we will "tighten" the energies to the candle in a clockwise direction, beginning with the "lightest" element, air, and finishing with the "heaviest" element, earth. Should you be into experimentation, practice both clockwise and counterclockwise movements (on different candles) to find which energy movement is most comfortable for you. Which one leaves you feeling good and empowered, and which one leaves you feeling dull?

Face the east with your feet slightly apart. With the candle positioned a bit out in front of you between the heart and solar plexus, move the candle in a clockwise circle, as if you are stirring a very large cauldron. Your movements can be small or exaggerated and free-flowing; however, they shouldn't be like a whirring blender. Nice. Slow. Easy. The purpose is to gather the energies of the quarter—in this case, air. Once you touch on what air is to you (the way it feels) and have set forth in your mind that you are "tightening" the energies of air around the candle, then try your best to reach "no mind." It may take several repetitions until you feel totally relaxed and "full." That's okay. If you are having difficulty reaching "no mind," then intone the sound "Aum," which is said to be the vibration of universal perfection and the touchstone of God/dess. After you have practiced this exercise several times you may wish to choose a finite number of "stirrings." The number of times you stir the candle depends on yourself and your desire. A good starting point is five times for change, seven times for movement, nine times for mastery, and twenty-one times for complete fulfillment. What works best for you is what you should eventually choose, however. You may have no desire to limit the times you tighten the energy around the candle—indeed, you may just want to go with the flow, and that's okay too. The only way you will know what is right for you is (of course) practice.

Once you have gathered the energy you feel you need, raise the candle slowly to the crown chakra (look upward) and bring it back down to the solar plexus (look forward). As you raise your arms you will be breathing in, and as you lower your arms you will be exhaling onto the candle. This movement has two functions: it instills your holy breath into the candle and, by movement, seals the air energies into the vehicle (in this case, the candle). Air represents prayers to heaven and in this small exercise you have requested that the smoke of the candle (its breath) becomes the breath of Spirit.

It is now time to move to the south, the next heaviest element. Rather than bip around the circle like the light-footed creature you are, try this instead. Step back onto the ball of your right foot and pivot a quarter turn. This will bring you immediately to face the south, with your feet the appropriate inches apart for balance. In this direction, we will be gathering the fire energies. Think

one

two

three

four

five

21

about the creative essence of the element. Acknowledge that you wish to put that energy into the candle. Take your mind to "no mind" and complete the prescribed number of clockwise stirring movements with the candle. Again, take a deep breath as you raise the candle to the crown chakra, and exhale as you move the candle down the meridian of the body to seal the fire energy into the candle. In this movement you have asked that the flame of the candle become the creative, powerful flame of Spirit. Done properly, you will begin to feel a very centered connection to Spirit and "no mind" may be easier to obtain as you proceed through the remaining steps of this exercise.

Stepping back with the right foot again and pivoting has us facing the west quarter, the element of water. When a candle burns it produces liquid; this is the flow of divine, spiritual energy surging forth to finalize your request. As with the east and south quarters, we are going to set in our minds that we are gathering the energies of the west quarter, water; and, as before, as we begin to stir those energies around the candle and tighten those vibrations to the barrel, we are going to move our thought process to "no mind." Once the stirring is complete, we again breathe in deeply, raise the candle, look heavenward, and then breathe out as we slowly lower the candle to fix the water energy. In moving from quarter to quarter and remembering to seal what we have just done, we continue to keep the body meridians balanced even though we have worked with different elements, one at a time.

Step back with the right foot, pivot to the right, and you are now facing the north quarter, the most stable and considered the heaviest of the four elements. It is from the north that you will fix the final earth element into this candle. It is on the earth plane that the candle will be used by yourself or given to a special friend for use. Having begun in the east with air, the lightest element (considered closest to heaven) and working down to the earth element

(what is closest to us), we have gradually pulled the elemental energies to the earth plane, where your desire will manifest into corporal reality. Thus, although north is the most important element when
it comes to manifestation work ("everything comes from the
north"), it is the last element to be invoked because it is the last
gateway from whence the manifestation must pass through. And, to
take this further, to manifest on the earth plane, we must have
worked through the gates of each element, one building upon the
other—which means that all elements are equally important, although not readily seen.

Again, without hurry, set in your mind what this candle is for,
what the element of earth represents in terms of energy, and then, as
you stir the candle, let yourself move into "no mind." As before, to
complete the empowerment, raise the candle to the crown chakra
and look heavenward; as you breathe out, lower the candle to the
position directly in front of the heart chakra.

Step back with your right foot, pivot to the right, and, as you
do so, consider yourself entering the divine essence of the primordial universe—into the arms of God/dess. You will once again be
facing east. Rather than stirring the candle from side to side, this
time you will close your eyes and make three clockwise circles in
the air with the candle beginning at twelve o'clock and ending at
twelve o'clock, starting from the crown chakra, moving down to the
solar plexus and then back up to the crown chakra. As you make
each circle, pull the circles in closer to the heart chakra. Although
your hands (holding the candle) will stop making the circles, your
mind (you may find) will not! Allow your mind to continue to spiral into the candle until it reaches "no mind." Hold this as long as
natural. Take a deep breath. Breathe out slowly onto the candle. Your
very next thought must be a visualization or statement of what this
candle is all about. In this exercise, we have intended this candle to
be for auric cleansing. If you are new to the Craft or unsure of your

abilities, look straight at the candle and say firmly, "Auric cleansing." They are the only words you will have uttered (other than if you were practicing the "Aum") in this entire exercise. As in the beginning of this exercise, raise the candle to the crown chakra, bring it straight down to the earth, and then bring it up again to the solar plexus. You have sealed the entire exercise.

Put the candle down. Your empowering work with the object is now completed. Slowly raise your hands and cup them together over your third eye, then bring your cupped hands (still together) straight down over the meridian of your body. In one fluid motion, open your hands and allow them to fall gently to their respective sides, palms down. This closes the meridian and brings stabilization.

SPIRITUAL USE: Learning to breathe and move slowly and gracefully in tandem with your own spiritual body can literally change your destiny in a positive way, regardless of whether you are doing the magick for yourself or for a friend.

PRACTICAL USE: Working with the elements in this way brings greater focus into all areas of your magickal work. Although we used this technique for an aura-cleansing candle, we easily could have been empowering a conjuring bag (a bag filled with herbals, magickal trinkets, etc.) for a sick friend. The truly inventive aspect of this exercise is that no matter what you are doing it for, you are gathering and harmonizing the energies around you and aligning your own energy with the fresh, cleansing aspects of the breath of heaven and earth. Finally, if you do this exercise without the candle and place a mental energy ball between your hands instead, you have a unique way of calling the quarters for any spiritual ceremony. Think about it.

ENHANCEMENTS TO THE CANDLE EMPOWERMENT

You can add any of the following enhancements to your magickal candles:

- Dress the candle with a magickal oil of your choice.

- Carve magickal symbols into the candle with a stylus.

- Paste a picture on the outside of a candle's glass container.

- Load a candle with herbs by carving a small hole in the bottom of the candle and filling it with herbs. Carefully seal shut with lighter flame. For safety reasons, remember to burn this candle in a pot.

- Add a pin halfway down, inserted into the candle. When the flame reaches the pin, the major force of the gathered energies is released. This technique is used for specific empowerments that are based on a particular timing factor.

Preparing an Auric Cleansing Water

Many cleansing techniques incorporate tools in which researched historical magickal associations (otherwise known as correspondences) are used to enhance the experience and boost the ultimate outcome of the working. Such tools may include herbs, liquids, gems, candles, etc. This recipe for auric cleansing water is to be used immediately upon blending, as the formula has no preservative feature, so it is not recommended for bottling. Use dried herbs (no older than a year, as it is thought herbs lose their magickal properties after a year's time). You can also use fresh herbs right from your garden or local greenhouse, if you so desire. These herbs were chosen specifically for their cleansing properties. If you were going to do a spell or working for money, then choose herbs whose correspondences relate to money, action, success, and abundance. Rather than a crystal, if prosperity was your focus, you might choose a lodestone or perhaps three tonka beans.

As with the candle empowerment exercise, it is up to you to choose whether you wish to cast the circle, create sacred space, or simply envision yourself surrounded by white light. There is much to be said about working within the magickal circle, and I do encourage it. For the auric cleansing water, you will need the following ingredients: White or clear glass (not plastic) bowl, ½ gallon spring water, ¼ ounce chamomile, ¼ ounce lemon verbena, ¼ ounce lavender, ¼ ounce lemongrass, one quartz crystal, one empowered white candle (as shown in the previous exercise), one sliced lemon, one rattle, one white altar cloth, and one bell.

Note: For this exercise, a white taper candle works best and should be empowered in the way set forth in the auric cleansing candle empowerment instructions.

To begin, place all your supplies on the white altar cloth. Pour the half gallon of water into the bowl. Be sure that the bowl is large enough that the water will not slosh over the sides, and that it is not too heavy, when filled, as to be cumbersome. Pick up the bowl and take one step backward from the altar surface. Hold the bowl just a little below the heart chakra and slightly out from your body. Slowly move the bowl from right (east) to left (west), then from up (north) and down (south) and back to center. Facing the east, slowly push the bowl out and away from yourself, envisioning that you are handing the bowl across an invisible curtain of energy. On the other side of the curtain is perfect love and perfect peace, the primordial energies of the universe. You are instilling this water with that energy. Pull the bowl back to yourself and as you are doing so, say, "Blessings of Spirit be upon you."

Step back with the right foot and pivot slowly (so you don't splash any water). You are now facing the south. Move the bowl across the invisible barrier into the primordial essence and back to yourself, speaking the words of blessing. Imagine that you have captured the pure energy of the unmanifest in the molecules of the water. Step back with the right foot again, pivot, and do the same at the west; then, finally, follow the same procedure facing the north.

This beginning sequence is an excellent training vehicle to teach students to "slow down" when employing magickal practices. Quick movements move the mind out of the alpha state, throwing one back into beta. Although this isn't a horrible thing (we operate normally in beta), you will reach better magickal results if your brain waves remain in alpha. Alpha is also very natural to the human condition. Your mind is in alpha when you watch television, drive, daydream, or are completely bored.

Move the bowl once again from the right to the left, and then from the crown to the solar plexus, returning to the center of your body. Place the water on the altar. Hold your hands over the herbs and the crystal (you can do this separately or together). Envision your hands filling with white light. Mentally transfer this light to the objects underneath and say, "May you be cleansed and consecrated in the name of the divine presence. Blessings upon you." (You can also use words that focus on the deity of your choice, or simply say "in the name of the Lord and Lady.")

Place all the herbs and the crystal into the bowl of water. Pause. Take three deep breaths and relax. Ring the bell three times. This helps to clear the air and lets all who are present know that the next stage of empowerment is about to begin. Hold the auric candle empowered in the previous exercise in your hands, close your eyes, and go to "no mind." Once you have reached this point, open your eyes and light the candle.

Pass the candle flame over the bowl from east to west (right to left), then from top (north) to bottom (south), and return to the center. Use the bottom of the candle to stir the water in a clockwise direction. The number of times you stir the water directly relates to the number of revolutions it takes for you to go to "no mind." You can intone the "Aum" sound to help you get there. Some practitioners prefer a favorite magickal chant, which works just fine.

When you have finished stirring the water, raise the candle to the heavens with both hands. Look up and to the left as you say, "From the heavens . . . ," then lower the candle straight down to the floor as you say, "to the earth," then move it back up to hover over the water. It is natural, at this point, for your hands to feel very hot and your inner body to be filled with a great sense of power. Let it happen. You won't explode. With one quick motion (fast is okay here), flip the candle and plunge the flame into the water, saying, "As above, so below. This water is empowered!"—or say nothing at all if the words do not come easily; just remember to keep the intent. As you plunge the candle into the water, you should feel the spiritual fire within yourself exploding into the water. Take a deep breath and step back. As with the previous candle exercise, put the candle down. As you next inhale, cup your hands over your third eye. As you exhale, bring your hands down slowly over the meridian of your body to the solar plexus, allowing your hands to separate and swing out to your sides, palms now facing the floor. Take another deep breath, exhaling slowly. This exercise is concluded.

SPIRITUAL USE: Once again, the slow movements, the focus on the directions, and the practice of combining energies harmonizes and brings balance to the self and helps to create an inner alchemy of dynamic, positive change. Making this particular water is a sacred journey into the realm of the primordial ebb and flow of the universe in an effort to obtain not only balance, but cleansing as well.

PRACTICAL USE: Once the water is made, its only limit is your imagination (although you cannot drink it). Use it in house blessings, spellwork, and ceremonies and rituals of all kinds. Fill small cotton bags with additional raw empowered herbs and dip in the water to sprinkle over the body for a complete cleansing.

How to Make White Blitz

On occasion you may run up against something that you consider fairly evil and insidious. You might be dealing with a stalker, a series of nightmares, or a run of bad luck. Granted, practical applications, such as notifying the appropriate authorities, delving frankly into your own psyche, or being smart and distancing yourself from negative people (a no-brainer that we often overlook), would be the first and foremost moves in a variety of situations; however, once again, we cannot ignore the value of the cleansing process. White blitz is a ground powder that can be linked to charms, talismans, words on paper, and even photographs. The powder can be used in a spell-working or a complete ritual environment. Its main purpose is to banish negative energy, which is why I have included the formula in this chapter; however, it does rely on magickal timing. If you are unfamiliar with this topic, which includes the phases of the moon, magickal days, and/or planetary hours, you may wish to look up the information in my book *Solitary Witch* or a book of your choice that covers related data (for moon phases and planetary hours information, see this book's appendices).

The formula is made in two stages. You will not need the white cornmeal for the first stage. As it is believed that spirits cannot tolerate salt, this powder can also be used for your ghostbusting endeavors, should you have the need to exorcise that sort of thing! And, in true folk magick form, should you feel the need to tromp around a graveyard, carrying this mixture in your pocket in a white conjuring bag sprayed with lilac water (lilac is a ghostbuster scent) is thought to keep errant and bored spirits from following you home.

For this formula, you will need thirteen eggs, a white disposable towel, a bowl, sea salt, three small mirrors the size of your thumb, an auric cleansing taper candle, auric cleansing water, three cowry shells, and a cup of white cornmeal.

Wash the eggs, the mirrors, and the cowry shells with the auric cleansing water made in the last exercise. Break the eggs into a bowl. Keep the shells out and lay them on a white, disposable towel. Throw away the egg yolks and whites (or use them in a cake or make egg sandwiches later, as you will not have done any magick with the mixture or fouled the eggs in any way).

Wash the eggshells carefully in clear running water. Set in the sun to dry. When the eggshells are devoid of moisture, crush them with a mortar and pestle in a counterclockwise movement (sometimes called widdershins in the Craft community) until you create a very fine powder. This, I warn you, will take some time. Rather than allowing your mind to drift over a compendium of thoughts while you grind the shells into powder, breathe deeply and evenly, centering your thoughts first on white light, and then "no mind." Some practitioners intone their favorite empowerment chant or simply make the "Aum" sound to help them stay centered and calm. You will only know what works best for you by experimentation. Above all, try to stay away from screaming babies, whining dogs, and pestering household members. Although many methods of magick can be done quite well amid the chaos of everyday living once you become accustomed to how things should "feel" to you, items to be used for cleansing purposes should be created in as peaceful an environment as you can manufacture. Honest. Once the eggshells are ground, set all supplies aside until:

- You can devote approximately fifteen minutes of your time to the empowerment process, and

- You can take advantage of a waning moon (for banishing energies), or

- You can take advantage of a Saturn planetary hour (for banishing energies), or

- You can empower the mixture on a Saturday (banishing day).

In physics, to create something we need nothing. Literally. No mind. (Some occultists like to say "empty mind," but I can't relate to the phenomena that way—it sounds like a derisive comment.)

In the white blitz recipe, the "nothing" becomes perfection, and within perfection, negativity cannot exist. White blitz, then, is a banishing tool, a protective tool, a vehicle of transformation, and a tool of ultimate balance. To take this further, thinking of that liquid light exercise you did, let's look at a quote from K. C. Cole, from *The Hole in the Universe*:

> Say the universe is made of vibrating strings; if you take away all the energy, the strings don't vibrate, but you still have strings. Or, let's say "nothing" is the watery universe of a fish. If all the energy is taken out, the water freezes. Instead of an amorphous fluid, you now have the crystal structure left behind when all the energy is removed. But it is still water. This structured kind of nothing corresponds to the vacuum in which we (and everything in the universe) ultimately reside.[2]

In the auric candle exercise we were visiting the world of nothing, grouping together a pattern of positive energy and directing that flow into the candle. Here, we want to take something that exists in one form, freeze it, and transform it. Now, the negative pattern is already "frozen" by the observer (you and probably anyone you've blabbed to, including those that you haven't blabbed to but don't like you anyway so they help to keep this pattern frozen; however, you are the captain of your own ship and if you don't like the pattern you have every right to do something about it—whew!). So! Our basic mission, should we choose to accept it, is to unfreeze the negative pattern and refreeze it into something that is more acceptable to us.

2   Cole, K. C. *The Hole in the Universe: How Scientists Peered Over the Edge of Emptiness and Found Everything.* New York: Harvest, 2001, page 16.

Because we are not the main character in the *Matrix* movies, we often use physical vehicles to assist the mind in getting to the "launch" position where we can affect the change we desire. Such tools include candles (which have been scientifically proven to affect the aura, by the way), plants, symbols, spoken words, etc. The vehicle we are using here, the white blitz, is designed to assist us in orchestrating a new pattern to affect and replace the old one. We want to destabilize the negativity so that we can rearrange the negative pattern into something more acceptable. Given that the strings of the negative event are still there (which is why we are making the white blitz), what we want to do with the white blitz is freeze those strings of negativity and make them react in a different way, which will create a whole new pattern. To accomplish this feat, we have to enter the realm of "no mind." Remember, in quantum physics, when a pattern is observed it freezes and changes character in direct relation to the thoughts of the observer (supposedly), which is why your teacher stresses and stresses and *stresses* the need for secrecy in your work of enchantment. The more you blab, the more chance of delaying your original work and, worse, of allowing it to be blown to bits by the thoughts of someone else. Likewise, you can feed those negative strings with worry, fear, and denial, which will make them vibrate stronger against you. There's much to be said about self-actualization and cleansing procedures. Hmm . . . contemplate that one for a while!

Now that we know what we're doing (sort of, because no one has yet come up with the complete answer and is talking), let's go on to finishing the white blitz recipe. Gather all your supplies and wrap them in a white cloth, including a cup of white cornmeal. Go outside to a place where you will not be disturbed. With the white cornmeal, trace a foot-wide circle on your back porch, in smooth dirt, or on your patio. Then, with the cornmeal, draw a line from right (east) to left (west) through the center and a line from the top of the circle (north) to the bottom (south) of the circle. (Refer to the Spirit Circle illustration on page 34.)

We are using the cornmeal for two reasons: its correspondence to North American history and goddess references as a symbol of plenty and its association to the manifestation of a three-dimensional item on the earth plane: corn. Therefore, we are using this natural item to create a circle and a vortex (the equal-armed cross) as well as to make references to the "as above, so below" magico-religious theory wherein the items on which you will be working are encased in an observable area (the circle); you are the only observer. At this stage you do not realize the true power you possess because it is here that you are the only observer. As long as you focus on the intent and touch with "no mind" what you wish to create, manifestation—unless it is truly against the will/perfection of the universe—will occur. It is from this point on, however, after the ceremony, that your working could jump the rails either because you have spoken of it to someone else or because your work is somehow seen in the interim and filled with negativity. For example, let's say you made this white blitz recipe for a friend who is having difficulties. If the friend is a magickal one and believes what you tell them and uses it privately, then the white blitz will most likely work. This faith, knowledge, or affirmation of knowing will strengthen the formula. If, however, your friend only half believes, tells someone else about the product who makes fun of it, or it is seen by an extremely negative member of the household and is mishandled in any way, the original strength of the recipe is reduced and perhaps destroyed. You see, ego has no place in magick. When you enter "no mind," there is no ego and therefore no blocks to the working. Once ego enters the picture as an observer, all can be lost. Yet there is that little Rule of Three thingy . . . all workings eventually propagate balance, and sometimes balance can be a dreadful thing. Think about it. Given this explanation, then, it would be unutterably stupid for anyone to work negative magick. There is

A Spirit Circle made of cornmeal creates a circle
and a vortex (the equal-armed cross).

no power in evil; there is only the self-gratification of ego. This is not the avenue of spirituality or perfection. We often become angry because we feel helpless in a given situation. Anger leads to ego-oriented action, which can be our undoing. So, if I told you that everything you want to do *will* work as long as you do your best to follow the rules of science, anger is no longer necessary because you are no longer helpless, which means the ego is no longer a factor. It is through repeated practice of meditation and magico-religious techniques that confidence is gained. This confidence leads to faith, which eliminates the ego. Do you understand?

Yet we are trying to get this formula done, aren't we! Okay. Place all items within the Spirit Circle with one addition: a clear glass of water that has been offered to each of the directions, beginning with the east and finishing with the north. You can do that right now and then place the glass in the circle with the rest of the items. If you like, offer the auric cleansing candle to the four directions as well. Light the auric cleansing candle (made like the one in the previous exercise—again, a taper is best for this particular working). Put the candle in the circle to the left (near the west). Hold your hands over the herbs (which represent the earth), the cowry shells (which stand for male/female and balance, as well as the sea), and the mirrors (which are associated with reflective capabilities and "as above, so below"). You can, if you like, add a crystal to the mix. We now have the earth element represented by the herbs, the water by the glass of water, the fire through the vehicle of the candle, and the air through your holy breath, which we will get to in a moment.

Mix the salt, eggshell powder, mirrors, and cowry shells in a clear glass or white bowl, situating the bowl in the direct center of the circle. Sit comfortably either cross-legged or kneeling, whichever is best for you. Take three deep breaths, inhaling and exhaling slowly. Inhale, raising your arms slowly up over your head and cupping your hands as if you are holding a beach ball. As you exhale,

one

two

three

four

five

35

bring the ball down past the third eye, past the throat chakra, and down to the heart chakra. Slowly rotate your hands so that your right hand is on top (holding the mythical ball) and your left hand is on the bottom. Reverse hand positions slowly, as if you are turning the ball in your hands. Keep rotating the ball until your fingers tingle and your palms grow warm.

Slowly move the ball of energy over the top of the Spirit Circle. Close your eyes and go to "no mind." Hold this as long as possible, then simply drop the ball by placing your palms flat toward the circle. Open your eyes. Envision everything in the Spirit Circle glowing with pure white light. In this formula, the white blitz is "fed" the pure water from the glass—just a few drops are sprinkled to the right, then the left, above, and below. Sprinkle only a tiny bit in the center—a flick of a drop is all that is necessary. Some practitioners also feed rum to the white blitz formula for a faster-acting vehicle. That is your choice. The formula is sealed by licking the thumb of the right hand, then moving the thumb from the left to the right (west to east) and then from top to bottom (north to south) over the Spirit Circle. When the candle has burned completely, the rite is completed. As salt collects moisture, package the formula as quickly as possible.

White blitz is a folk magick application. It is not considered to be in the realms of high magick, but falls within the auspices of shamanistic energies. Regardless, its root is quantum physics and the process of making the formula can be an amazing teaching vehicle in itself.

Complete Aura Cleansing Ceremony

The complete working requires the following supplies: ceremonial white sage, coarse sea salt, a magickal oil designed for good fortune and invoking positive energies, a new white cord that is five feet long, two white illuminator candles (which can stand for the God and Goddess—matter and antimatter, sun and moon, particular saints, Spirit, etc.), frankincense resin (which can be burned, simmered, given as an offering to deity—your choice, so you will need the appropriate vehicle; in this application it is soaked in a bowl of spring water with a crystal), aura cleansing water (as shown in a previous exercise), and an aura cleansing taper candle (as explained earlier in the text) for each individual who will be present. Therefore, your ceremony requires two rites (to empower the candles and make the aura cleansing water) previous to its application. You will also need an appropriate clear or white bowl for burning the sage, ½ cup rosemary, ½ cup hyssop, ½ cup lavender, and small white cotton bags for each person. Absolutely necessary for this ritual are a dozen carnations (if you are working solitary) or at least six carnations for each participant in the ritual. Flowers for each individual present adds a nice addition to the ritual and ensures that negativity is not passed from one person to the other.

Place all supplies on your altar (or flat nonflammable surface). If you choose to use an altar cloth, it should be white. Place one illuminator candle on each side of the bowl of auric cleansing water. Close your eyes and breathe deeply at least three times, more if you are stressed or feel too many things are weighing on your mind. It is here that you ask your ancestors and deity for assistance in this working.

Continue by taking three deep breaths, inhaling and exhaling slowly, and sounding the word "Aum" deeply and slowly. This vibration helps to cleanse the body and calls the perfection of the universe through cosmic waves. When you feel you are ready, hold your hands over the white rope and say, "Energy and pattern of the earth, I cleanse, bless, and consecrate thee in the name of Spirit." Dip the rope in the water. Use the rope to sprinkle the water at the quarters. To manage this feat, you may wish to either (a) transfer some of the water from the central bowl to a smaller bowl, or (b) if you are doing this ceremony with another person, have them carry the bowl and you sprinkle the water. Moving in a clockwise direction and beginning with the east, sprinkle a little water and a little salt on the ground around the area you will be working (or on your altar if you do not plan to move). Move to the south, the west, the north, and finish again in the east, then sprinkle a bit of salt and water at the center of where you will be working.

Next, hold your hands over the ceremonial sage and say, "Creature of the earth, I cleanse, bless, and consecrate thee in the name of Spirit." Light the sage (be sure to have a fire-safe bowl in which to carry it). Blow softly on the sage three times, saying, "Energy and pattern of sacred smoke, cleanse and consecrate this sacred space and spiral my prayers to the center of manifestation!" Carry the sage around the room to cleanse the area in a clockwise direction. Pass the smoke over yourself and anyone present. Pass the smoke over the altar and the illuminator candles. Dot the illuminator candles with a bit of your favorite magickal oil. Hold your hands over the candles and say, "Pattern of wax and wick, I cleanse and consecrate thee in the name of Spirit! May your blessed light bring joy and power to this working." Light each candle, saying, "Wax and wick, flame and smoke, powers of peace I now invoke!" (You can also say the name(s) of deity, saints, angels, powers, etc.)

Pour the bottled spring water in the bowl. Place the bowl on the center of your altar. Hold your hands over the frankincense and crystal and say, "Creatures of earth, I cleanse and consecrate thee in the name of the divine presence. Bring higher vibrations to this working!" Place the frankincense and the crystal in the bowl of water. Point to the bowl and say loudly, "I charge thee to attend this working and magnify the power of this ritual!"

Put three drops of your favorite magickal oil in the herbal mix that consists of the hyssop, rosemary, and lavender. Crush the mix with your hands, saying, "Creatures of earth, I cleanse, bless, and consecrate thee in the name of Spirit! May all you touch turn to peace and joy . . . become . . . be one!" Breathe deeply and close your eyes as you repeat "become . . . be one" several times. Imagine you are at the center of the universe and filled with light. Then say, "Perfect love and perfect trust; Spirit [or you can say a deity name] enter now with us." If there are several present, then all should repeat the words several times until harmony is felt in the room. Circle members can sing or drum during the following steps.

Position the rope in a circle, end to end, making the circle shape with the rope. Sprinkle the center of that circle with auric cleansing water and the dried herbs in the bowl. Have the first person step into the inner circle. (You will remain outside this inner circle, as will everyone else—only one person in the inner circle at a time.) Choose six carnations and dip the heads in the auric cleansing water. Shake lightly, then sprinkle the person in the inner circle with the flowers, then brush the flowers from the top of their head down to their toes on the front and back of their body (something much like it is often done in spiritualist ceremonies). This action of brushing the flowers over the body is to remove all negativity. If static electricity is present on any one person, then this person is doubly blessed by the gods during the procedure. Break the flowers and throw them on the floor outside of the inner circle. Have the person jump out of the circle onto the broken flowers to break any last negative connections and dispel the negative energy. As they straighten their shoulders and step off the crushed flowers, hand them an auric cleansing candle with the instruction that it is to be burned as soon as they return home. If you are practicing this ceremony alone, light your auric cleansing candle now and, as you inhale, hold the lit candle aloft; as you lower the candle to your solar plexus, exhale slowly (don't blow out the flame), visualizing all negativity leaving your body. Allow the candle to burn completely on the altar.

Put broken flowers in a discard bag or bowl. If you are cleansing several people, this ceremony is best done outside. The person who picks up the flowers to dispose of them must wash their hands with clear spring water after they pick up each batch of flowers.

Choose three more flowers and move to the next person. When everyone has been cleansed, take the last of the flowers and sprinkle the altar. If you are alone, cleanse yourself and then sprinkle the altar with new flowers. Remember, do not ever dip the flowers back in the bowl once they have touched someone. When everyone has been cleansed you have the choice of closing the ceremony or moving on to an additional rite, such as giving offerings to deity or raising energy for a specific working. The stage has now been set for any type of ritual, from a handfasting or wiccaning to general healing, a high holy day, esbat, or other magickal endeavor. If you choose a simple spell, cleanse, consecrate, and bless a candle in a particular color, place it on the altar in an appropriate candleholder, and continue your working. When you are finished, remember to thank the gods and the ancestors and thoroughly clean the area. Leftover herbs can be placed in the cotton gris-gris bags and given to participants to take with them.

This particular ceremony is extremely useful and can be massaged in a way that fits your beliefs and your taste in ritual. It is an excellent addition to your collection of healing arts and techniques because, frankly, you can never do enough cleansing!

Summary

In this section we discussed the importance of cleansing, meditation, auric programming, and learning to actively incorporate various techniques to open yourself to a more spiritual lifestyle. Designed to take you from moon to moon, these exercises have been an incredible help to me as well as many of my students in dealing with life's daily challenges. May they be of assistance to you as well.

one

two

three

four

five

41

TWO

Exercises in This Section

The Sacred Journey

Life is your greatest teacher if you are willing to learn, and although sometimes we may eagerly stand there at a quarter in a ceremony and ask for transformation from the Morrigan (big intake of breath from some readers who have wide eyes and are shaking their heads vehemently and saying no-no-no!) or stand confidently in front of our High Priest and Priestess (who will most likely fall off that teetering pedestal you are requiring them to stand tippy-toe on), or simply kneel alone at our altar focusing on the powers that be, saying, "I'm ready! Teach me!"—when the lesson comes calling, the experience is often ensnared in an unpleasant life circumstance, perhaps unrecognizable as our original wish (some students never do get it), invariably presenting a situation that you truly don't want to deal with. Not all lessons are uncomfortable or so veiled, but usually the big ones are. How we work through the problem determines whether we are afforded the opportunity to dance that tune again or if we have learned the complete symphony and now can move on to something new.

Life is the sacred journey, there is no doubt about it. Teachers, friends, and family members can point the way, but only you walk down the path. This path consists of integrating what you have learned, how you process that information, what you do with the results of your lesson, and how you observe and manipulate that lesson into your world. Time and again I have heard students and practitioners in our community complain that advanced material is not available or that a particular teacher is not "fulfilling their needs." Such declarations indicate that the student has donned a particularly heavy pair of horse blinders. It is not the quality of the teacher but how *you* have progressed through the experience, because quite frankly, sometimes Spirit throws lousy teachers at you on purpose. In truth, it is only when the student realizes the true import of the journey that he or she is ready to progress to a more advanced level of working. When the personal advancement occurs, it is done *sub rosa*, beneath the rose, under a veil of self-imposed secrecy, because that is what the student will come to understand as desirable for successful personal fulfillment.

It is thought by some modern occultists that ancient symbols, such as the pentacle, the spiral, the star, the rose, the braid, and the knot, represent patterns on many levels—the corporal (a star is a star is a star), the spiritual (the thought energy evoked or transformed when working with the corporal object), and the alchemical form, which can be both a philosophical and a real-science quantum physics pattern. The very first recorded symbols appear to be combinations of the five basic elements, which include a straight line, a curve, spirals, and the dot. Hands, hearts, and footprints were the next to grace walls and caverns, followed by the pentacle and the sunwheel (or equal-armed cross encased in a circle, sometimes called the Spirit Circle), amid other interesting shapes and pictorial representations. In this chapter we are going to deal with several occult-related symbols and how you can use them to further your personal spiritual journey through rite, spellwork, meditation, and ritual, with the focus of becoming one with deity.

Your Foot Upon the Path:
The Pentacle and the Rose

The pentacle and the rose are virtually the same symbol viewed in different contexts. The pentacle is the iconographic representation of the elliptical path of the planet Venus in the heavens and is one of the oldest known symbols traced by humankind. Known as the Evening and the Morning Star due to the planet's path in the heavens, the pentacle/Venus has been used in a variety of iconographic drawings in numerous cultures. Due to the number of petals in a real rose and how the petals naturally grow, this lovely flower quickly became associated with the pentacle, which opened a large array of occult associations, including purity, secrecy, love, the divine mother, beauty, happiness, heart energy (the source), grace, and one's adventure into the unknown. Pythagoras and his students employed the pentacle as a representation of the sacred harmony of the mind-body connection; the ancient alchemists and the Gnostics used the pentacle as a symbol for quintessence *(quinta essentia)*.

In alchemical study, the rose is shown in the colors of red and white—light and action—representing the necessary duality that is bridged to create a whole. Early Christian iconography likens the rose to the Goddess, which created the title "Queen of Flowers" and became the symbolic essence of Mary, Queen of Heaven, thus folding back upon itself to the precursor, the pentacle. Sophia, too, finds her place here, as she is the goddess of alchemy, after all! Whether hinting at the Divine Proportion to becoming a stylized version in the Egyptian ankh (where here the pentacle and the rose have become the key to life), the pentacle/rose is considered a symbol of mastery through change. In medieval mystical traditions, the rose (and variations thereof) represents the pathway to enlightenment—a compass for navigation once you have knocked upon the door of the sacred crossroads.

Your personal navigational course is definitely a divine mystery and must be traversed with secrecy so as not to invite the negative thoughts of others into your inner sanctum (another symbol of the rose and a rule of quantum physics), represented by the language of the rose, the essence of mystery. The natural spiral growth of the

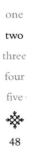

The number of rose petals can relate to levels of one's study as well as the magick of numbers: five equals change; six "as above, so below"; and the Rose Compass, an extension of the four-petaled rose, is a navigational tool of the eight winds.

rose is nature's way of showing us how all things mature. All four symbols—the star, the pentacle, the rose, and the spiral—are linked to the divine feminine and the motion of change.

In the occult, the number of petals shown in the symbolic rose relates to levels within one's study as well as teaches the student the magick of numbers. The four-petaled rose relates to the four elements, the four corners of the earth, the four watchtowers, stability, etc. A rose with five petals (change and using the five elements to create change) thus becomes the microcosm. The six-petaled rose is the macrocosm. Twenty-one petals? Divine mastery. The Rose of the Winds is the Rose Compass—the navigational tool of the eight winds and an extension of the four-petaled rose.

The center of the rose is the void from which all things grow: the primordial soup; the place of possibility where all things can become. It is *nigredo* (the first state in esoteric alchemy), a place that speaks of the necessity of change . . . which we'll touch on a bit more later in this book.

The Ceremony of the Rose

The ceremony of the rose is a ritual written to assist the practitioner as they navigate along the difficult path of spiritual advancement. It can be utilized by the student when they feel ready to advance their sacred journey or take a step onward and upward in their occult studies. It is a wonderful way to connect with deity, find a new aspect of spirituality that speaks to you, or help you get back in tune after you've been "out of wack" a bit.

You will need the following: one white stock candle, magickal oil—rose or mint scented, ¼ ounce dried mint, ¼ ounce dried rose petals, ¼ teaspoon powdered copal resin, ¼ teaspoon powdered frankincense resin, one powdered rose quartz stone, clear water, incense, candleholder, incense holder, five fresh roses, pen and paper, mortar and pestle, and a mallet and scissors.

Consider your goals as you crush the herbs with the mortar and pestle. Copy one of the rose designs from page 48 as it applies specifically to what you are seeking. Carefully write the goal you have selected on the back of the rose/pentacle paper. Dot the paper with the rose-scented oil. The idea is to find as many occult correspondences as possible that speak to the physical senses—the feel of the rose petals, the fragrant scent of the rose, the beauty of the flower to the eye, and so on. Cut your goal paper into tiny pieces with the scissors—the smaller, the better—and add it to the herbal mixture. Grind thoroughly with the pestle. When finished, empty the mixture into a clean white bowl and place it on the center of the altar. Put the rose quartz stone in the bowl. Light the incense and carry it around the area in a clockwise direction. Pass over the bowl containing your magickal mixture.

Next, rub the candle lightly with a small amount of rose- or mint-scented oil. Sprinkle with a small amount of the ground herbs—not too much, as you don't want the candle to become a flaming torch. Light the candle. Pass the flame over the bowl in a pentacle design. Now, there are several ways of drawing a pentacle: there are pentacles for the directions, for the elements, for invoking and banishing without the compendium of whatevers . . . so I suggest you use whatever comes naturally to you. Here, I'll describe drawing from the top of the pentacle down to the left, up right, across left, down right, and back up to the top. Place the candle beside the bowl. If you have fresh roses, encircle them around the bowl.

Most practitioners, especially in groups, are used to being very active during ritual—there is drama, movement, etc. Here, we are taking a different tack. Sit in a rocking chair facing the bowl and candle. Relax and breathe deeply several times. Close your eyes and think of your point of origin. Merge this into a feeling of relaxation and creativity. Continue to move this feeling out from yourself and into the bowl with your mind. See the goal rise from the bowl. Hold this visualization as long as you can.

Remove the rose quartz stone and place it beside the candle. Take the powder/paper mixture outside. Beginning with the west, throw a bit of the mixture to the winds, asking for peace, tranquility, and clear knowledge of the right way to reach your goals. Turn to the east, moving clockwise, and repeat. Turn to the north (only moving clockwise) and repeat; now to the south, only moving clockwise, and repeat. Hold the remaining mixture in your hands and lift up and to the left. Say (and mean it), "In the name of the sacred rose, my work shall manifest in the best positive way for me. So shall it be!"

Inside, move the candle onto the center of your altar. Make the sign of the equal-armed cross in the air over the candle and at the same time make a sound that moves from your toes up through six of the seven chakras and let it go out of your mouth. This is a way to seal a spell so that it freezes in time to protect your work against the unfoldments of a negative nature. As long as you tell no one about your work, it should be successful. Allow the candle to burn completely. The ceremony is done. Place the rose quartz stone and petals from the roses (if you had them) in a gris-gris bag (a magical bag made of cotton, velvet, or flannel). Seal it also. Carry it with you until your work manifests in the physical.

The Sacred Knots of Mastery

There are several ancient references to magickal knots, from the Gordian knot mastered by Alexander the Great—who did the unthinkable and simply cut the complicated affair with one swift whop of his sword—to legends of Witches using knots to raise and calm ocean winds, but what few truly contemplate is the significance of the pattern that the knots create. In this exercise we are concentrating on the figure eight or the sign of infinity and how it relates to the actual practice of magick—the waves of what cannot be seen.

Read that last sentence again.

Underline it.

Highlight it.

Study it.

Yes, that interesting sigil means "eternity"—but how is it used? In *Solitary Witch* I showed you how, through quantum physics and the light cone, the cone of power in Witchcraft is actually raised. Here we're going to talk about what to *do* with that power. Let's work on an exercise to help you master this incredible sigil.

Energy Waves

When most people cast a circle or work with energy they usually visualize one of two patterns: the straight line (sending energy out or receiving it in linear fashion) or a ball of energy (as when you gather energy between your two hands into a pulsating sphere). In this simple exercise I'd like you to review how you currently manipulate energy and tweak your visualization a bit. Rather than seeing a straight line or a ball, do a wave. We know that energy, light, and thought travel in waves; if we are to enhance our personal power through visualization, then it makes sense that we match the natural patterns of the universe as closely as we can—in this case, through the wave.

Soft, flowing music works extremely well with this exercise. You may wish to choose a particular musical piece to listen to before you begin. Stand straight with your feet slightly apart. Take three deep breaths. Raise your arms to touch the heavens, then slowly lower them down to touch the earth. Return to the standing position with feet slightly apart, hands in a prayer position over your heart chakra. Again, breathe deeply at least three times, allowing any stress from the day or evening to drift away from your mind and body. Now close your eyes and envision your auric body filled with white light, which will slowly seep into the physical body. You may feel lighter or have a sense of relief or freedom. Slowly move your right arm out in front of you, and as you do, visualize energy (white light) leaving your right hand in waves. Consider this a prayer, if you like, for the less fortunate than yourself. Bring your hands back to the prayer position and take three more deep breaths. Now move your left hand out in front of you with the duplicate wave visualization of sending energy out. Take a deep breath and return to the prayer position.

Next, put your right hand out and envision white light and positive energy waving *into* you (rather than projecting *from* you). Repeat with the left hand. Take a few moments to contemplate the following:

Which hand felt more powerful at which stage? Does your right hand pull better than your left? Or is it the other way around? Next, after three deep breaths, put both hands out and visualize energy pulsating from yourself into the universe in waves of light. Again, think of prayers for the needy. (Every little bit helps.) Move your hands back. Take a deep breath. Move your hands out again and "receive" waves of white light energy. Believe that these waves carry happiness, harmony, good health, and peace. Note how you felt during this process. Finally, to the music if this helps, slowly move the right hand out in front of you, send waves, and catch that same energy with the left hand and bring it back toward you. How did that feel? Try it a few times to get the momentum. Now send out with your left and retrieve with your right. When you are finished, put your hands up to the heavens, then down to the ground, then clasp them in front of you in a prayer position. This exercise is concluded.

Practice this exercise three times a day for one week. Be sure to write your results in your personal journal. Take note, also, of how your life may be changing this week and how the exercise may be affecting daily activities.

one

two

three

four

five

54

As this drawing shows, manifestation occurs by drawing from above and below, merging energy in the pathway of the infinity sign (as appears over the magician's head).

The Infinity Sign in Magick:
The Enchanted Knot of the Universe

In the standard tarot deck the infinity sign, that famous double loop, is poised above the head of the Magician (left). His card means "making thought into form," a realm of mastery and manifested intention. You cannot master anything if you are stuck in negative thought patterns, and the Magician reminds us that we must set aside the time to actually *do* the work. The Magician's card often depicts elements of alchemy, like the snake, the eagle, and the lion, which match both elemental compounds as well as esoteric manifestations. Let's look at the sign of infinity in the light of magick shown in the illustration on page 56. Rather than viewing the sign on its side, we're going to do a bit of creative thinking and turn it on its end, now becoming the representation of the double helix, the staff of Hermes, and the Voudon vèvè for Damballa and Ayida Wedo. The simplistic version of the double helix is, of course, the uroborus—the snake that eats its tail. In the occult, the snake is really the light wave, which is, in fact, the seat of wisdom, the carrier of information, and the ultimate condenser of manifestation into the earth plane. Your DNA, shaped like the double helix (the infinity sign), carries all the information about your physical body, and there is debate that it may also be imprinted with elements of your auric body as well (that which survives after death). Read the remarkable stories of current transplant patients to learn more about this phenomena. There is much to contemplate! Finally, if you look at the Egyptian ankh (the key to life), you will understand that it is truly the key to magick as well.

The first part of this exercise is to review the diagram given on page 56 and then meditate on it. This is also an excellent tarot card spread (if you are good at that) and works well with the runes (should that be your choice of divinatory tool). You are the direct result of your memories, your past actions, and the events that oc-

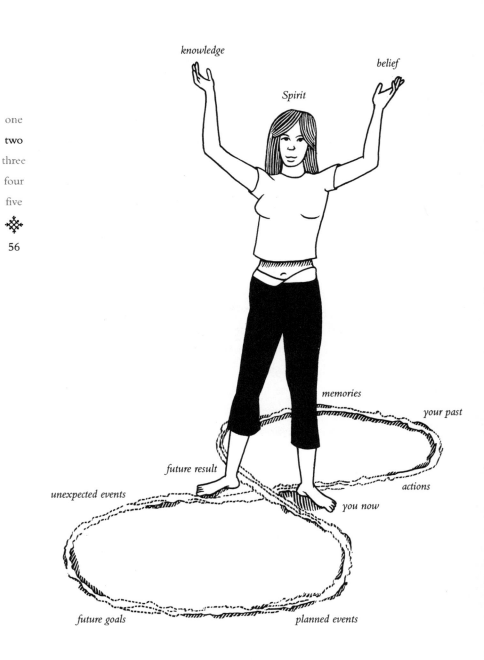

The infinity diagram: you are in control of your life!

curred in the past, as illustrated in the diagram. What makes your future and your present is your knowledge, your belief, and your companionship with Spirit (whatever you believe that to be). Your future consists of your plans and the actions you will take to fulfill those goals, the direct result of past actions (which are sometimes unexpected), and the combination of these two forces, which often brings the unexpected (although it really isn't if you think about it). If you become caught in a negative scenario (for example, your best friend just torched your life and it is all you can think about) then, according to this diagram, that one-track-mind negativity is going to directly affect your future because you fed it with your pain, unhappiness, and feelings of failure (you trusted them, you stupid schmuck). You forget that you are in total control of your life and therefore, inadvertently, you turn the path of magick against yourself. Because we know that time is not linear, it is extremely important that we concentrate on gathering a momentum of positive thoughts, actions, and goals as much as we possibly can. By performing magickal applications to increase harmony, spirituality, and the betterment of ourselves and others, we are actually changing the fabric of the cosmos as well as of our own future (which is also the present, and indeed our past). Remember, magick and life are unfoldments of energy patterns, and you are in control of those patterns, whether you realize it or not. You are in control by the choices you make, the magick you do, and the actions you take. Think about it.

Now that we've reviewed the possible meaning of the sign of infinity, let's try using it. After studying the diagram closely, take out your favorite divination tool and use the diagram like a spread. Place your chosen runes, cards, or magick stones (whatever you use) on the diagram and read the divinatory pattern. You can use a test question first or go for the gold, choosing a question or problem that has been plaguing you. Have you gained additional insight? Try using this spread for others. Professional readers may find this diagram extremely helpful at psychic fairs and in private readings.

Using Infinity in Spellwork

Having seeded your brain with the diagram, meditation, contemplation, and divination, it is time to move on and incorporate infinity in a magickal working. Although there are many creative ways we can incorporate the quantum pattern of infinity, we'll start with a candle and gem magick application with several ideas for enhancement. We'll focus on spirituality and the quest for enhancing our communication with our higher selves—because when that flows smoothly, all other things fall into place. Again, the pattern lends itself well to all types of workings, including healing, the physical manifestation of bringing items toward you (like a car), and even diminishing debt. The technique can be used in a group circle environment for raising energy and even incorporated in full moon and sabbat themes, given the number of items needed (8). For now, we'll concentrate on forging a strong, pulsating path to inner advancement.

Crystal Eight Spell

This is a spell of self-mastery. You will need a smooth, flat surface that can hold eight burning candles; three cups of sea salt; parchment paper, pen, and magickal ink (optional); mortar and pestle; eight snow-white taper candles or votives and their respective fire-safe holders; incense of your choice: sandalwood, frankincense, copal, or myrrh lend themselves well to spiritual pursuits (stick, cone, or resin, your choice)—white sage sticks also work well; eight crystal points (best) or rolled crystals; one piece of amethyst (the nicer the better, but use what you can afford); a taglock representing you (a bit of your hair is best, a photo is second best, a printed astrological birth chart is a third option—or use all three); holy water; magickal oil; and a set of new dice.

Write your full name on one small piece of parchment paper. Attach taglock and place it in the center of the altar. On a different piece of parchment paper, write your goal—an example might be

"Smooth communication with my higher self and Spirit" (or the Goddess or a particular deity). Burn this piece of paper in a white fire-safe bowl. Grind the ashes with mortar and pestle. Add them to the sea salt and mix thoroughly.

On the flat working surface, carefully make the infinity sign with the salt/ash mixture. Make it large enough that a candle and a gemstone can be placed at each significant point, as shown on the diagram. The loops should cross over your taglock. Make sure the line of salt is unbroken, adding more salt if you don't have enough once you get started. As you are drawing the infinity sign, begin your chant that relates to the purpose of the working. You may wish to use the following: "Salt and ash, review the past, choose the loop for which I ask."

As our lives consist of many loops of choice running concurrently at any one time, the focus here is to choose the one "right" loop that will open the way for the accomplishment of our intended goal and strengthen the energy of its momentum for future manifestations. Keep repeating this part of the charm until the salt infinity sign is completely finished. Indeed, our lives are a braid of energy, loop upon loop, as the old Celts tried to tell us!

Roll the dice to determine how many days you should repeat this spell, given the theme you have chosen and your preliminary work. The number on the dice directly relates to the number of consecutive days you will work this spell, repeating the chants, etc. Your number of days will be from one to twelve. Double numbers—snake eyes, double sixes, double fives, etc.—indicate a very successful conclusion and also give you a hint on how many days (or months) it will take for your intent to begin showing signs of success. Double ones equal 24 to 48 hours. Leave the dice where they fall on the altar surface.

Light the incense. Put three drops of scented oil in your holy water. The oil will float unless you use an emulsifier. Some occultists choose to add this blending agent where others do not; the choice is yours. Once mixed, sprinkle water around the outside of the figure-eight pattern without touching it, then pass over the incense or sage wand in the same manner. Move these items clockwise around the pattern, repeating this part of the chant: "Water and scent, cleanse intent; sacred smoke, Spirit invoke."

This step is to ensure negative thoughts from yourself or others are not currently influencing your choices, and that these stray or intended thoughts stay away during the magickal process.

Arrange each of the gems at the eight points of the diagram, naming what they stand for as you place them. If you are using points, arrange the points so that they flow clockwise along the salt pattern. As you "fix" the points and name them, keep the following chant going: "Flame and gem bring power in; force to form, energy blend."

Arrange the candles next to the crystals and light them one by one, building power as each flame springs to life—begin with the candle in the center and move clockwise around the pattern, repeating the above chant. When you are finished, sit back and take three deep breaths. Connect to the divine with a "waving" energy motion within yourself. Close your eyes and relax. Contemplate what you wish to accomplish.

You have now set the matrix for your working, generated sacred space, called on divinity through the use of elements, and are ready to fully raise the energy to complete the working.

Hold both hands out in front of you, palms facing the working. It is time to repeat the full chant in direct respect to your abilities: if you are new at magic, nine times (or more!); of medium ability, seven times. Been at this a long time? Try three at first, probably only once if you are really an old pro. As you chant, literally move the upper part of your body in a figure-eight motion. Too, the number of times the chant is said can also be equated to the magick in numbers, and even if you know precisely what you are doing, you may feel it necessary to say that chant twenty-one times! Go with your gut.

"Salt and ash, review the past;

choose the loop for which I ask.

Water and scent, cleanse intent;

Sacred smoke, Spirit invoke.

Flame and gem, bring power in;

Force to form, energy blend.

Spark to light, future unfolds;

As I say, the magick holds!

Desire, weave this tapestry;

As I will, it now shall be!"

one

two

three

four

five

With the end of the last line on the last chant sequence, pound the altar with your right hand (not so the candles fall down) and make a guttural sound from the depths of your diaphragm to "freeze the moment" of the final wording. The working is finished. Allow the candles to burn at least two hours. Snuff them out, never blow. You can use the same candles the following days for as many as the dice indicate; when they burn out, replace them with new until all the days have been completed. If you can, leave the pattern in place until your desire has completely manifested, or sweep salt, gems, and taglock into a gris-gris bag, dot with magickal oil, place on your altar and burn one white candle by the bag each week on the same day, intoning the chant once. Spray the bag with magickal spray or white rum and pass over the living flame to "reheat" (not too close!).

Infinity

There are an infinite number of ways that you can employ the infinity sign in your work now that you know exactly what it means (and your mind will lead you to much more). Placing eight drummers at the points shown on the diagram makes for an interesting ritual to raise power. You can use eight different drumbeats or begin with one drum beat, like a round, always moving clockwise. If you orchestrate a large ritual, forget the circle—do the infinity pattern with the people; it is guaranteed to make for an interesting experience. On a smaller scale, place a representation of a holiday or a phase of the moon at each point. From macrocosm to microcosm, fashion something by hand in the figure-eight pattern (clay, photographs, wood, beads, etc.)—you can even make a miniature talisman once you have done the first ritual and are familiar with what is to happen when, why, and how. If you want to work with the dead, replace the salt but not the holy water (unless you are working with Voodoo, and then they have their own requirements). Salt repels the dead (so they say), yet you need the empowered water to keep strange things from floating in where they are certainly not wanted. Finally, if practiced enough, you won't need the props. Then you will find that life can be most interesting, indeed!

Witch's Pentacle Talisman

An excellent exercise in contemplation, meditation, creativity, and empowerment is to work with the various magickal symbols in your own unique way. The Witch's pentacle talisman on page 64 is perfect for both beginners and advanced practitioners due to the fluidity of the energy. This talisman was designed to teach students how to recognize the symbols in the drawing and name them and then take a field trip outside to see how they might be duplicated in natural surroundings. The drawing is also a power matrix of its own and can be activated in a variety of ways, using candles, gemstones, pebbles, seeds, etc., at various points on the drawing. Rather than using a copy machine (which is easy, I know), it is far better to use magickal ink and parchment and have each student re-create the drawing on their own, sounding out the various symbols and contemplating their unique energy. The symbols in this drawing include the seven classical planets; the sacred spiral; the elements of earth, air, fire, and water; the pentacle; the infinity sign; the symbol for the

Goddess; the antlers of the God; the symbol for alchemy; the stylized Eye of Horus; the Sacred Circle; as well as several Reiki healing sigils, should you choose to journey on that path. All of these symbols can be found if you surf on the 'net and will mean much more to you if you discover them for yourself. If a single symbol eludes you, then this is a sign that you have been ignoring this energy in your life and you must make the extra effort to determine first what that symbol stands for and, second, how it can be integrated into your spiritual workings. Although I gave a complete walk-through of the infinity diagram earlier in this chapter, the Witch's talisman and its integration into your life is up to you to work through. Every student needs to tackle a challenge or two! Once you have determined what all the sigils mean, you are prepared to go further in your studies by working the seedbearers of light exercise, which can be turned into a complete ritual on its own, if you so choose.

Seedbearer of Light Exercise

For this rite you will need the following: gold or silver cord; magickal ink and pen; parchment paper; seeds—sunflower seeds for success, fava beans or tonka beans for prosperity, white beans for family stability, etc. (The type of seed bears directly on the theme you choose, and the number of seeds depends upon how many of the symbols you wish to activate by direction. Use a selection of seeds and coins if you need fast cash; a combination of mustard seeds and moonstones for increasing wisdom, intuition, and divination skills; or rose quartz and amethyst gems for healing body, mind, and soul.)

Re-create the drawing with parchment and ink, considering the theme you will use for this talisman and for this working. On the parchment, encircle the talisman with your name written as many times as it will fit in an unbroken circle. Place each seed/gem on the sigils you plan to use, activating these points by using your imagination as you speak. For example, "Fire for the flame of spirituality. Earth for the stability I need in my life. Hands of power for

Witch's pentacle talisman.

protection and healing," etc. The associations you make are built on your knowledge of the symbol and your personal need. Light the candle. Pass the candle over each activated sigil, whispering "birth" to each point. For example, "The birth of stability, the birth of protection, the birth of knowledge," etc. Allow the candle to burn for two hours (or completely). Once the candle has completely burned —whether today or on the last successive day you choose to work—push the seeds/gems to the center of the talisman. Encompassing the items, roll the paper toward you if you are bringing something into your life or away from you if you are banishing a particular energy. Tie each end tightly shut with a gold or silver cord. Dot with wax to seal, and then seal magickally in your own style. Put in a safe place and watch the magick in your life blossom and grow!

Spirit Will Teach You What You Most Need to Know

Witchcraft is divine alchemy—a philosopher's stone for the modern world. You either have the courage to work with its transformational energies and look within yourself or you'll walk away (some people actually run—go figure). Your greatest test in the Craft is life itself and how you incorporate the occult teachings you learn as you are presented with the results of your own previous decisions. Whether you believe it or not, Spirit brings you what you need to know to advance in your occult studies when you need it in direct response to your previous behavior and chosen life path. Your responsibility is to recognize what you need and accept the gifts given to you. (Ouuu, some people aren't going to like that one.) So this means if you study your brains out, try to act like a decent person, and pay attention to the opportunities presented to you, you're at least ahead of the game. However, if you are impatient, complain, throw a tantrum, sigh, scream at the heavens, cry, moan, grumble, pressure your High Priest or Priestess, treat others badly, proclaim yourself an expert or "godly" in person or on the Internet, and stamp your foot repeatedly . . . unless you have done the work, you're not going to get the advancement you desire *until you make the concerted effort through your own behavior and choices* (which must be positive in nature)—and the universe decides you are ready to handle it.

I could write reams, tell you every secret and every mystery (even if I knew them all, and I don't), to no avail. Why? Because it is Spirit that provides that "light bulb" moment, not me. Not your teacher. Not some cliquey, fake magick group on the 'net or some nut who has High Priestess Syndrome. Not anybody. Just Spirit, which circumvents human anomalies. I not only believe this, I've seen this repeatedly in action: Spirit teaches you what you most need to know when you need to know it. Have faith in that and you will always move upward and onward, regardless of the mess at hand.

Which is why Witches are different from the other guys—we realize that there are no middlemen (or women) to God. In my mind, a High Priest or Priestess of the Craft is a facilitator. They train to the best of their individual ability. You get the trainer you earn. That's the long and the short of it. Your teachers light the way, but they can't drag you onto the path. You have to move under your own steam . . . or fail. If you mess up? Fix it and keep on going. Experience is the best teacher. If the trainer messes up? Learn from the experience because you were supposed to! Don't wallow in it. Disengage immediately and keep plugging along. A new opportunity will present itself now that you have learned this lesson. A Witch—a true follower of our path—is courageous, if nothing else! Sometimes Spirit actually gives us crappy teachers because we are to learn what we are *not* supposed to do on our future life path. And honestly? If you had a really lousy occult teacher, or a horrendous boss, or a nightmare of a spouse, Spirit has very, very special things in mind for you. Live up to the expectation of Spirit, cut your ties to the negativity, and keep on going!

As magickal practitioners, we have lots of tools from the occult world to play with to help us advance at our own pace—practices that keep us entertained, learning, amused, and sometimes frustrated. From what goes on the altar to the intricacies of astrology, the special energies of each sabbat to what to do and not do in a ritual circle environment, to candlemaking, alchemy, oil blending, perfumery, herbal lore, self-hypnosis, drum trancing, gem work, making incense, sacred dance, blending powders, fashioning conjuring bags and crafting wands, stangs, staffs, and even ritual jewelry and clothing. Then there are talismans, energy workings, amulets, divinatory tools, writing, poetry, painting, the mechanics of the group mind, working with animals, totems, the astral plane, the dead, the deities, the airts, the quarters, the watchtowers, dragons, gnomes, faeries, sylphs, salamanders, undines . . . whew! Honey, if you're bored, you've got a problem!

All these wonderful, nifty-neaty things (and there are more, I just hit the surface) can and should be used for the express purpose of divine creation. Now what is that, exactly? Basically it means using your will to manifest, in your own way, items and thoughts of positive intent that strengthen the overall harmony of the universe. Well! That was a mouthful, wasn't it? As I see it, we have only two fat flies in the ointment of life—ourselves (we can be our own worst enemy) and other people.

You know, when I first entered the magickal world, I thought it was really lame that a bunch of Buddhist monks would live in a monastery, away from the world, and spend their days chanting, burning incense, and gazing off a mountaintop. "Stupid," I said. "Worthless," I thought. "Escapists! They should be out there pitching in with the rest of us."

Until, *duh*, I realized that we *have* to have them.

The universe needs them to do what they are doing, just like it needs you to elevate your own spirituality so you can do what you need to do. We all affect the warp and weave of the world; do you want to enhance the quality of life, or do you want to put it in the toilet? You have a choice, you know. Really . . . you do. And you make those choices every single day. Honest! The problem is, we make so many choices that we aren't always sure which ones were really the heavy hitters and which ones were inconsequential. With occult studies, however, forewarned is forearmed, especially if you learn to take the time to educate yourself thoroughly on at least one divination system. And, it is no lie that the longer you are involved in the esoteric, the more you will understand—as long as you keep working at it and trying to learn new things.

Practicing Witches—the real ones—learn the value of everyone eventually. It just takes some of us a little longer than others.

However . . .

Glittering analogies aside, we ain't sittin' on a mountaintop, you and I; for whatever reason we've chosen to throw ourselves into the daily grind of jobs, partners, children, marriages, divorces, coven dynamics, small towns, big cities . . . But fair warning: we can also lose what we earn by the continued choices we make. Who needs hell and the threat of fire and brimstone when you've got your own actions to haunt you?

Scary, isn't it, when you *really* realize you are the master or mistress of your own fate, and that the devil isn't a person—it is ignorance.

Ritual of the Talking Head

Ancient tribal humans, in their quest for power and information, would stick the heads of their ancestors or enemies on poles, hoping that the world of the unseen would unfold its great mysteries by proximity. Grisly and unnecessary, there are other ways to honor our ancestors and still gain the information that we desire. Originally designed for a Samhain application, it can be used at any time of the year. If you have a pressing question and need a speedy answer, you might wish to try this simple ritual. The symbol on page 70 is one you are familiar with—the skull and crossbones.

For this ritual you will need the following: a pencil and paper; five pennies; two white candles and candleholders; one crystal; a magickal oil of your choice (mint or lavender work well); one glass of water; one lemon; three tablespoons white sugar; one gris-gris bag; your petition; spring water; and this talking head herbal mixture—grind (or mix) the following herbs together: wormwood, mint, broom, orris, eyebright, marigold, and myrrh. Add five drops of patchouli essential oil to one cup of herbal mix. Do not ingest.

Draw the crossbone design on a piece of paper. Place the paper in the center of the working area. Acknowledge the four quarters by sprinkling spring water at each quarter. Circle each quarter once with one lit white candle in a clockwise direction. Do not light both candles, just the one.

Place the lit white candle on the table. Place the crystal on the left side of your skull and crossbones design.

Write on your petition exactly what you want to know, whether it is solution-oriented or a desire for information on a particular subject. Anoint the paper with a bit of the magickal oil. Place the paper under the skull and crossbones design.

Put a small glass of water on top of your spell mat. Put one drop of lemon from a fresh lemon in the water. Sprinkle white sugar around the glass of water.

Anoint the crystal lightly (not much) with the magickal oil. Keep the crystal positioned to the left of the glass.

Anoint other white candle very, very lightly with magickal oil. Hold the candle in your hands and say, "From the depths of the universe, talk to me. From the sea of mind and mystery. Go to the place where the information I seek is available and bring it back to me." If

one
two
three
four
five

70

Skull and crossbones.

you have a time limit, place a calendar beside the glass on the left side and circle the day you need the information. (Just to let you know, if this doesn't work the first time it's because you need to practice using a calendar in this magickal way. Keep trying.) Light the candle. Circle the candle around the calendar (if you are using one) three times. Place the candle on the left side of the glass, above the crystal.

one

two

three

four

five

Sprinkle the crystal with the herbal formula. Do not breathe in the dust—it has wormwood in it, which is not good for you! Hold your hands over the crystal and repeat the same statement as you did for the second candle ("From the depths . . ."). Close your eyes, look up to the right (with eyes still closed), and imagine the crystal glowing with power. Open your eyes, draw them over to the crystal, and bring the crystal to your heart chakra. Take a deep breath like you are breathing in the information. Put the crystal back where you had it. Place five pennies, the herbal mixture, and the crystal in the gris-gris bag, adding the crystal last. Dot the bag with magickal oil. Keep to the left side of the glass of water unless you choose to carry the gris-gris bag with you (which is okay).

Go to each quarter and thank the gods.

Burn both candles each day for ten minutes until:

a) You get the information, or

b) The candle finishes burning.

The information will come to you in a variety of ways—so don't expect a missive to drop from the sky on your head like a golden hammer or materialize in front of your nose like in a fantasy story. Be observant. Listen! Look! Be patient. The solution or information may come in a dream, in a passing conversation with someone, a telephone call, over the Internet, etc. There are endless possibilities, but you must be open to receive the information. The key to this working, as when we discussed the symbolism of the rose, is secrecy.

The Witch's Claw of Protection

The next exercise entails analyzing the symbol on page 74 and writing your own spell or ritual of protection based on the symbology in the design and what you learn after the sign has been empowered. Although I provide standard empowerment instructions, the rest of the working is up to you. Good luck!

> *Der Geist macht das Verheilen. Sie machen das Denken.*
> The Spirit does the healing. You do the thinking.
>
> —POW-WOW

Supplies needed: a copy of the Witch's claw design; a candle; matches or a lighter; holy water; white sage; a fire-safe bowl; a black marker; magickal oil; sea salt; a black stone; a rattle; and magickal activation powder.

To begin, make your own copy of the sign. Place the sign on the ground (earth energy). Cleanse the sign with fire (a lit candle) in one hand and holy water in the other, rotating first counterclockwise and then clockwise. Light the white sage and blow the smoke softly across the surface of the sign. Sprinkle a bit of water at each compass point (north to south, then west to east). Allow the sage to smolder in a fire-safe bowl as you continue to work. With a black marker, write on the back of the sign exactly what you desire. You can use magickal symbols, code, magickal alphabets, etc., if you don't want anyone to know or understand the significance of the sign. This procedure is called "owning the sign."

Dot any points on the sign (star points, triangles, crosses, hearts, petal points) with the magickal oil, saying, "The perfect order of the universe now enters this sign. All positive potential is present in preparation for this working." You can now move the sign to your altar or leave it on the ground as you continue working.

Sprinkle a circle of sea salt around the sign. This is to keep all negative energies at bay while you work. Nothing evil can cross the salt barrier. Place your lit candle, for the moment, up and to the left of the sign. You are sending out to the future, which will some day become the past.

If you will use the sign as a mini-altar for this working, then all items should be placed on the sign from this moment on. If you are simply empowering the sign to hang in your home, place your items on the sign during the working and remove them after the enchantment is complete. Cleanse the black stone with sage smoke and holy water; use the stone to absorb negativity. Dot the stone with magickal oil and clearly speak its purpose. Tap it on the sign seven times and then place it outside of the salt circle so that it can begin working immediately. In thirty days (or if things have been particularly awful), cleanse the stone with salt, holy water, and sage smoke. Leave in sunlight (a Pow-Wow practice) at the height of the day for at least one hour.

Activate the sign by using a rattle. Begin at the center of the sign and work out, following the design as best you can. Each design falls into a pleasing rhythm. Do this three times, intoning your desire while you work. This is called "talking to the sign." Sprinkle the sign with a magickal activation powder.

Using the rattle again, repeat the following chant nine times:

> *"Out of the black and into the red*
>
> *Out of the red and into the white*
>
> *Out of the white and into the gold*
>
> *Out of the gold and into the world.*
>
> *From my hand to God's hand*
>
> *The magick is made."*

Note: "From my hand to God's hand" means to go from the collective unconscious into the three-dimensional world.

During this time the rattle should be moving in a clockwise motion around the sign, ending at the upper left at the end of each repetition. Look up and to the left, then begin the chant again.

Witch's claw of protection design.

If you desire to add any magick, such as an additional candle, petition, herbal mixture, etc., do that now. When you are finished, feed the center of the sign three drops of water and place the white candle over the water, then say the following with meaning in your voice:

"And it came to pass on this day that the Witch [or whatever you call yourself] *fully set up the tabernacle and anointed it, and sanctified it and all the instruments thereof, anointed them, and sanctified them, and blew upon it the breath of life."*

Blow softly three times on the sign, then say to seal, "Stern. Weit. Blau als Heaven. Hell als die Sonne. Wie ich verkünde. Es wird gemacht werden." (Meaning: Star far blue as heaven, clear as the sun, as I will, it shall be done.)

With great gusto, create a strong sound that rolls up from the tips of your toes and out your mouth and, at the same time, with your thumb seal the design in the air with an equal-armed cross. Then say, "Gods and spirits, I release you into the light to complete this undertaking. Peace be with you. So mote it be!"

If you need to add a healing to this working, you may wish to use the following:

GENERAL HEALING

    (used to "tear out" illness)

    Dieses Wasser und dieses Feuer

    Dieses Wasser und dieses Feuer

    Dieses Wasser und dieses Feuer

    Dies ist ein grosse Dinge

    In dies grosses geh eilige landen

    Unser shoene Frau Maria

This water and this fire

This water and this fire

This water and this fire

This is a deep thing

Go hastily into the ground

[pull out the illness with your hand and throw it to the
ground]

[In the name of] Our beautiful one, Maria

Note: *Maria* is the Latin word for "sea." It is highly possible this chant was referring to the void, therefore it would be "In the name of our beautiful one, the sea of God." "This water and this fire" are the alchemical addresses of change.

White Magick

Many of my books have been published in other countries, and within those cultures the words "white magick" are a necessity in the title due to that culture's collective view on magick and enchantment. I took a great deal of grief from American readers a few years ago, who scoffed at the terminology when it was used in some promotional material in error on the United States' version. It never occurred to them that America isn't the only place in the world where seekers may be interested in learning to master the unknown of the occult. This is a prime example that even in the Pagan community there will be those people who fail to look "outside the box." As you work through any occult-related material, remember that respect of all cultures and religions is an inherent requirement for obtaining our own Wiccan "perfect love and perfect trust."

As a direct result of this interesting behavior on the part of my own community, I created a "White Magick" line of products with the premise of purity in a harmonic design and a focal scent of lilac.

This White Magick set is an interesting concept based on light, energy, and patterns that you create.

First, redraw the White Magick pattern on page 78 on parchment paper. Artistic skill is not required. You can cheat and use templates from an office supply store if you like. Once the paper is prepared, you can begin working magickally with the design. As you draw, consider the shapes and the numerical associations.

one

two

three

four

five

THE SHAPES

Triangles—The power of three, the trinity of magick, and the cone of light.

Square (the snake design)—The four elements, the four directions, stability, and earth magick.

Circles—Purity and protection.

Stars—Change as well as the combined energy of human and element.

Swirls—Movement and fire magick.

Hexagons—Alchemical and ceremonial magick.

Zigzag—Flow and water magick.

Starbursts—Astrology and the magick of the stars.

Ovals—Spirit.

Bars—The dead.

Arrowheads—The future and air magick.

THE NUMBERS

One—Ultimate perfection and beginnings.

Two—Partnership.

Three—Communication and travel.

Four—Stability.

Five—Change.

Six—Talent and inspiration.

White Magick pattern.

Seven—Movement through growth.

Eight—Mastering your own talents.

Nine—Wishes and success.

Ten—Closing doors so that new ones can open.

When you are ready to work the magick, begin by dressing your white candle with just a bit of magickal oil and sprinkling the candle with a very small amount of magickal powder (see part four—powder is optional). Empower the candle by saying your desire aloud while holding the candle at your heart chakra. Feel your desire move into the candle (your hands will tingle or grow warm). When you feel calm and relaxed, place the candle in a safe holder in the center of the snake design. The snake stands for the movement of energy. If you desire, you can also put a written petition under the candle. Do not light the candle at this time.

Letting Spirit guide your choices, place small, natural objects, such as shells, leaves, gems, herbs, magick beans, feathers, or human-constructed items (small mirrors, metal charms, runes, lots, etc.), on the shapes that match your intent. The design works exceptionally well with quartz crystal points. You can place objects on only a few of the shapes or on all of them—the choice is up to you. When your pattern is complete and feels right, repeat your intent. Sprinkle lilac-scented water around the outside of the design to seal the intent, then light the candle. Let the candle burn completely. Leave the design with the objects untouched until your desire manifests. To protect the pattern, you can cover it with a new, clean, white piece of cloth—or, you can burn a white candle every day, repeating your intent, until your desire manifests. When your desire is met, give all the used objects to the earth with a "thank-you" and seal with a kind deed.

Healing for a Friend Using Magickal Symbols

Reiki is a channeled form of energy healing with origins in Japan. The word "Reiki" comes from Japanese picture writing, known as kanji, in which *Rei* means "spiritually guided" and *ki* refers to life-force energy. It is generally accepted that Reiki was rediscovered by Dr. Mikao Usui of Kyoto, Japan. He believed the system to be the ancient healing method of some of the world's greatest healers. Along with the training, Dr. Usui passed on the Reiki ideals, which are just as valid today as they were then: "Just for today, do not worry. Just for today, do not anger. Honor your teachers, your parents, your neighbors, your friends. Give thanks for all living things. Earn your living honestly." All who practice Reiki today can trace their lineage back through their instructor through one of the original twenty-two masters.

Reiki is not learned like other methods of healing. In order to perform Reiki on yourself and others, you need to have your energy "tuned in" to channel it. This energy transference that occurs between the master and the student is called an attunement. You can find such masters by visiting the Web with a search engine. There are quite a few! In Reiki, the practitioner draws upon the unlimited supply of universal life energy and pulls it in through the crown chakra and out through the hands. Even if you haven't had the benefit of an attunement, you can still use the magickal symbols provided in this exercise not only for healing but to manifest physical objects as well.

First, let's start with a brief explanation of the symbols used, and then on to the exercise itself.

Wedjat—One of the most popular ancient Egyptian amulets, used to protect the wearer and bestow desirable qualities, such as health and vitality. The wedjat eye, or Eye of Horus as it is sometimes called, can be drawn on anything you wish to heal or protect. This "eye" is a mathematical shorthand of fractional proportions for Egyptian medicinal ingredient measurements, listed in six parts. The eyeball is ¼, the eyebrow is ⅛, the portion in front of the eyeball is ½, the portion behind is 1/16, the curlicue is 1/64, and the line straight down is 1/32. In total, the picture equals 64.64, with Spirit supplying the last little bit to equal this number.

one

two

three

four

five

Hexagram—One of the most popular symbols in element magick is that of the hexagram, which is the fire and water triangles placed one on top of the other. Uniting the elements through this alchemical symbol coalesces force and form. The earliest examples of the hexagram date back to 700 BC. This symbol gives command over the four elements and stands for the fifth element, that of Spirit.

Cho Ku Rei—Means "put the power here." It is a sigil used in Reiki energy work. The symbol is used for calling in spiritual power, cleansing the aura, banishing negativity, and creating a receptive environment.

*Healing sigil illustration; clockwise from bottom center, hexagram,
Cho Ku Rei, wedjat eye (Eye of Horus), Cho Ku Rei.*

For the healing ceremony, you will need the following: white candle (pink and purple is fine, too); healing magickal oil; a copy of the healing design; incense; a glass of spring water; a clear glass bowl; a photograph of the person or animal to be healed; a piece of paper with the person's name written on it; a candleholder; an incense holder; a nail, pin, or stylus; two ounces of your own healing herbal mixture, and a muslin bag.

To begin, copy the design given on a piece of paper. As you draw, chant the person's name, followed by the "Aum" sound. Keep chanting as you create the design. Set aside. With the stylus, draw the Cho Ku Rei symbol on your candle; set aside. Pour the healing herbs you have chosen into a clear bowl. Place three drops of healing oil in the mix. Blend with your hands. Rub a few drops of healing oil onto the candle. Put one drop of healing oil into the glass of water. Set the candle above the Eye of Horus. Put the water to the right of the candle, then place the herbal mix to the left of the candle. Write the person's name who is to be healed on a piece of paper and place it in a cloth bag. Add a crystal or other healing gemstone if you so desire. Put the incense in a holder to the right of the design. Place the person's photograph on top of the paper in the center of the design. (If the photo is so big you can't see the design, put the photo under it.) Draw the Cho Ku Rei symbol in the air over each item. Envision the power coming down into your crown chakra and moving from your hands onto each item to empower and activate it to your desire. Take your time.

Light the incense and pass it over the picture. Visualize healing energy permeating the individual's aura like fragrant smoke. Pass the incense over the bowl of herbs. Light the candle. Intone the word "Cho Ku Rei" as you move the candle over the picture, then pass it over the herbs. Place your finger on the Eye of Horus and draw a line in the air from the eye to the picture. Ask for strength, protection, and harmony for that individual. Draw a line in the air from the hexagram up to the picture. Ask for the power of the elements and Spirit to make the individual's environment safe, healthy, and secure. As above, so below. Finally, draw the Cho Ku Rei symbol in the air over the picture of the person. In your mind, create a magickal eraser and, with eyes closed, use the eraser to wipe out any disease in the body or mind of the person. Take a deep breath and open your eyes.

The visualization for the last part of the spell may be difficult if you have not practiced visualization techniques. Practice is really all it takes. You are going to make the Cho Ku Rei symbols spin. Imagine the bars of the Cho Ku Rei symbols swinging inward, toward you, like a gate opening. They will continue that swing to complete a full circle. As they do, each Cho Ku Rei symbol will rotate—the left one in a clockwise motion, the right one in a counterclockwise motion. Begin spinning them slowly, then allow them to go faster. As they do, keep repeating the word "Kriya" (meaning the combination of the Cho Ku Rei symbols). You will feel the energy rise. When you feel it has reached its peak, visualize this energy surrounding your hands and the picture. Slowly lower your hands to the picture and say (and mean it), "The healing is done! It is complete!" Place the herbs in the muslin bag. Dot the bag and seal it with the Cho Ku Rei symbol in the air over the bag. Give the bag to the sick person to keep with them or place it on your altar by the individual's picture. You can work in this manner every day until the person is healed.

Astrological Symbolism

We can't leave this section without giving reference to astrological symbolism. These signs, symbols, and glyphs equating to mathematical proportions of the movement of heavenly bodies represent an incredible system so simple, yet so complex, that one never tires of the subject. From self-analysis to event planning, to studying the patterns and the dynamic energy associations, there is much there for the interested student to learn. The last exercise in this section, should you be so brave as to tackle it, is to memorize the data listed below and incorporate this information in a spell specifically designed for your spiritual betterment. Good luck!

TERM	TYPE	SIGIL	BASIC ENERGY PATTERN
Aries	Zodiac Sign	♈	Beginnings and action
Taurus	Zodiac Sign	♉	Manifestation and security
Gemini	Zodiac Sign	♊	Movement and mental energy
Cancer	Zodiac Sign	♋	Emotions and home environment
Leo	Zodiac Sign	♌	Success and courage
Virgo	Zodiac Sign	♍	Analysis and service
Libra	Zodiac Sign	♎	Beauty and socialization
Scorpio	Zodiac Sign	♏	Regeneration and justice
Sagittarius	Zodiac Sign	♐	Idealization and study
Capricorn	Zodiac Sign	♑	Building, business, and rewards
Aquarius	Zodiac Sign	♒	Humanitarian and group work
Pisces	Zodiac Sign	♓	Spiritual and visionary pursuits; transformation
Sun	Planet	☉	Success
Moon	Planet	☽	Emotions
Mercury	Planet	☿	Communication
Venus	Planet	♀	Socialization
Mars	Planet	♂	Action
Jupiter	Planet	♃	Expansion
Saturn	Planet	♄	Order
Uranus	Planet	♅	Experimentation
Neptune	Planet	♆	Transformation
Pluto	Planet	♇	Regeneration
Juno	Asteroid	⚵	Marriage and partnerships
Vesta	Asteroid	⚶	Hearth and home
Pallas	Asteroid	⚴	Wisdom
Ceres	Asteroid	⚳	Creativity and regeneration

Chiron	Comet	⚷	Healing
Dragon's Head	North Moon Node	☊	Expanding life path in a positive direction
Dragon's Tail	South Moon Node	☋	Constricting a pathway
Conjunction	Aspect	☌	Combining two forces
Opposition	Aspect	☍	Mediating two forces
Square	Aspect	□	Creating challenge
Trine	Aspect	△	Harmony
Sextile	Aspect	⚹	Opportunity
Semi-sextile	Aspect	⚺	Mild support
Inconjunct	Aspect	⚻	Delays

Summary

Whether you are just starting out in the world of enchantment or have been here for quite a while, the first two steps (represented by parts one and two of this book) still apply. Practice the fine art of cleansing on an as-needed basis and periodically check where your feet might be on that path to spirituality through the continued practice of exercises, rites, rituals, and spellwork focused on that purpose. Spirituality isn't a "once and done" business—it is a growing, blossoming vortex of energy within yourself. In this part I gave you several major concepts to work with—the pentacle and the rose, focusing on your sacred journey; the infinite crystal empowerment material that urges you to look at manipulating energy in a different way; the Witch's pentacle, a unique talisman for planting the seeds of success in your life using your level of knowledge and your personal creativity; and the White Magick concept. Finally, we worked with a familiar symbol that is not necessarily magickal—but is, in its own way, mysterious (the skull and crossbones)—and provided a protective symbol for you to analyze and build into your own working. I deliberately chose methods from different cultures to remind you to always look outside of the box.

THREE

Exercises in This Section

Tending Your Spiritual Garden

"No eureka moment. No epiphany—just a series of psychic gearshifts that manifest themselves in . . . carriage and tone of voice."[1]

As Within, So Without

Just as an earthly garden needs constant attention, so, too, does our spiritual garden. When we first begin our journey of spirituality our garden is filled with all sorts of interesting items—it was not, after all, a fallow place before we sought to investigate what might be there and what we could possibly put in it. Everyone's spiritual garden is different, because each individual is unique and each person has specific goals related directly to them to accomplish—yet, as we are all human, we do share some commonalities, and our energy connections to each other become a vast and endless wellspring of possibility.

Working on our own spiritual garden is one of the toughest jobs assigned to us while we are on this plane. It just ain't easy. Throughout life, lots of things crawl into our garden—misconceptions, emotional debris, broken dreams, errors in judgment, you name it. The analogy of a spiritual garden came to me one summer when my father was very ill. He is an avid gardener and has a series of raised beds in which he plants vegetables and herbs. The spring had been extremely wet and without being tended, due to his illness, the raised-bed garden turned

---

1. Mike D' Angelo, "Two Amigos," *Esquire*, March 2004, page 76.

into a sea of thistles and nettles. The family realized that the sad shape of the garden made my father extremely unhappy, so we set about pulling, clearing, and eventually planting the beds.

Like new students (and pay attention, old hands, this also applies to you) looking out over that ocean of nettles and considering our task was, needless to say, mentally daunting. We knew the soil was good (gad, the nettles were big enough) but to rid the area of those prickly nasty things without using a weed killer (that's the easy way, but would adversely affect the soil), we had to get in there and clear it weed by weed. And so we did.

Our spiritual garden, when we begin, is much like this. We go through it, misconception by misconception, old trauma by old trauma, and begin to eradicate what is not useful to us by utilizing tools that are sometimes new—meditation, visualization, the practice of energy manipulation, increased introspection, behavior modification (by this I mean diminishing and removing bad habits under our own direction), etc. This process can be extremely painful (try grabbing a handful of nettles and see what that feels like!) and the time it takes to do this is not less than twenty-four hours. Depending on our current situation, background, level of understanding, body chemistry, and how much we are willing to rise to the challenge of looking within—well, this can take quite a while. The good thing about our spiritual garden, just like a real one, is that you can see progress right away if you are observant. By being cognizant of our steps forward, we can give ourselves the needed boost to keep going, even when that one root of that one nettle is very thick and very deep. Eventually, we learn the expertise of how to remove those big weeds, and the clearing process becomes easier.

Like a real garden, our spiritual garden needs tending. There are several dangers here that I have personally witnessed with one's spiritual garden. Once we manage to clear the debris, it is highly possible for one to become too inflamed with the proposed image of our own newfound power. This creates a whole new kind of weed that grows at a phenomenal rate and often explodes the group mind (should you be in one), as I mentioned earlier in this book, and it puts our spiritual gardener back at least ten paces in life (trust me, I've seen it multiple times). Then, there is the gardener who, once he or she has cleared a lovely area, becomes lonely for old patterns (those thistles really weren't that bad, and they do—on occasion—have pretty flowers) and allows everything to grow back again as it once was, and then bemoans the fact that this has occurred. Teachers who help you clear your garden once are not so inclined to do this a second time. Finally, many times we make the "first pass," clear out most of the top garbage, and forget that when we pulled pretty hard at some of those weeds, they actually broke off—we didn't get at the root. Then comes a planetary retrograde that applies to the energy of that root and—oops, we're back in the saddle again!

For those of you who have been involved in magickal studies and spiritual advancement, there is yet another hurdle you must overcome: expanding the garden. You reach a point, you have an epiphany, you sigh in happiness and joy, and so you let the garden go (just for a little while) as you focus on a particular life issue, rather than keeping it weeded or trying to expand it. Perhaps you use a few of the tools you were taught, or perhaps the situation is so encompassing that you let go of what could help you most, mentally blocking the new skills you have learned. When you come back to the garden (if you get back)—you guessed it—the garden is choked with new weeds choking what you have so carefully planted.

We've talked about the weeds, but what actually goes into a spiritual garden? We can plant a new belief system, encourage the growth of inner harmony and outer understanding, and allow self-love to blossom and progress from within, where it will eventually affect our physical environment in a positive way. We can sow seeds of confidence, brother- and sisterhood, patience (I'll repeat that: patience), creative skills (such as singing, drawing, painting, poetry, stories, etc.), and learning to know when things are really not about you. Sometimes we simply try to own garbage that doesn't belong to us, you know? Therefore, think twice before dragging an unusual, funky item into your garden—it may catch your eye, but not for what you first intended. It could be a (gulp) plastic gnome with a "lesson" inside.

Learning to Read the Signs

Enlightenment appears to be difficult to obtain not only because this state is so hard to describe but also because of the way each person is built—that state (it would logically follow) would not be the same for everyone. Perhaps our error lies in assuming that enlightenment is standard, like 10,000 of the same make and model of a car. On the surface, of course, all those cars look alike—but they are not. I might buy the same make and model vehicle as you have, but yours might last longer, and in mine the transmission drops out after two years. This is why, I think, structured religions are born, live, and die. We have a vision of nirvana but, as we are all human, everyone's vision is a bit different—for a time the group mind can create a single vision, but if it does not match the pattern of the universe in a healthy way, exactly, precisely, and it doesn't attempt through actions, words, and thought to grow toward that perfect match, it will cease to serve its purpose. If we do not maintain our personal spiritual garden, then we cannot create patterns of positive change, either alone or in a group, and we will never blossom into all that we can be.

When a crisis occurs in our lives, Spirit drops hints of who, what, why, and how a successful solution can be activated by scattering pearls of energy everywhere; if we pay attention we can read these glittering signs. The whispers of assistance are all around us, yet we often don't hear them because we haven't attuned ourselves with the realization that help is already there. This information is constantly in motion. It only freezes and solidifies when you recognize it. That is science. Our emotions cloud our vision, causing a knee-jerk reaction that pushes the solution farther away than it was a moment ago. That is the effect of our own control and biochemistry. The solution doesn't come rushing in on a white horse—it has always been in place. That is quantum physics. You just have to "push de button." If your spiritual garden is relatively clean, then the button won't get stuck and will ignite the solution. If your spiritual garden is filled with weeds, that solution-oriented button will most likely get stuck or detonate what you didn't intend at all!

That button's hardwiring is put into place by you. It could be prayer, positive thought, meditation, and the mental reliance on Spirit that all things will go as they should—representing the elusive word "faith." If you have hardwired the button to negative emotions, then the solution you desire may turn into a negative outcome. Too, if the button is in good working order because you have been tending to your spirituality, then what might be disaster to one person will be a mere blip on the emotional scale for another.

Some scientists say our world is made up of ten dimensions, and the newest in string theory quotes the number as eleven (mastery). Scientists have been playing with the string theory for about thirty years now, and there's a new theory on how the universe works (but totally untested)—brane, which actually equates to the magickal number seven (three-dimensional brane suspended in a four-dimensional bulk)—it will be interesting to see where they take that one in the future. However this discussion jumps us to an interesting place, but not entirely applicable to the work at hand.

The string theory, mathematically tested and supported by experimentation, although not conclusively, says that there are three dimensions we can see. The fourth equals time. The remaining six (or seven) are invisible to us, yet constantly touch us. Perhaps there are far more—but we, as humans, can only postulate as far as we can fathom at any given time and can recognize only what we wish to weigh and measure.

To explain: Hold up a pencil. You can see the pencil; what you can see are the three dimensions. Yet what it takes for that pencil to manifest goes beyond what you can see—envision, if you will, a string attached to the right and left ends of the pencil, as if it were suspended in the air. Now that is quantum physics. And that is magick. Your peripheral vision is mysticism (and science). It is mysticism only because they haven't been able to weigh and measure it . . . yet. The more you become attuned to the wholeness, the more enlightened you are. The more enlightened you are, the more you will see in your personal peripheral vision, and this is where signs come from. This is where that "knowing" comes from—those threads that go beyond the end of that pencil (or car)—and this is where the sign of infinity fits neatly into place. The center, for the purpose of this discussion, is the dimensions you can weigh and measure, and the loops are the strings that vibrate to make the item in the center manifest, whether it is something as amorphous as love or as solid as a car.

If, for example, we wanted to manifest a car, the car is in the center—it is not the beginning or the end result, it is the composite of a pattern that appears in the three dimensions that we can see and measure with scientific machines. It takes the manipulation of energy through all the dimensions to create that car, and the creation of that car (since the world is such a busy place) occurs through the path of least resistance. What appears to take so long is our perception of time and the blocks we have already created through words, actions, and deeds—and our belief is predicated on those. If we let go and believe that time truly does not exist, that motion truly does not exist (very difficult), that we are quite capable of instant manifestation (as particle physics has already taught us), and if we have not mucked up the entire thing with stupid stuff, then, theoretically, that car could be manifested instantaneously by using one's thoughts to create and manipulate the proper pattern. Therefore, one's thoughts would be that missing percentage in all those calculations, as they travel faster than the speed of light and, like gravity, are not affected by time. We already know that one's thoughts can affect a controlled experiment—that the observer can make or break a scientific study or a spell.

Our thoughts, then—your thoughts, my thoughts, your brother's thoughts—would equate to the dark energy of the universe (called dark only because it is mysterious; this appears to be a metaphor in the scientific community, I didn't make it up)—morphing into the collective unconscious, that totally ethereal .000001 percent that is fourteen times more powerful than anything known.

Each dimension, it is said, has rules of government—Newton's old theory of order, which applies, but now has changed into something a bit different. A worm hole, then, might not be a hole at all, but a pathway of least resistance. If the scientists who are plodding along to properly measure and the mystics who are equally toiling to properly live by getting rid of emotional baggage ever combine their expertise, our world will be a different place overnight.

If we have grown sufficiently, we learn to read the signs afforded by the other dimensions. Whether we are talking about particle theory, string theory, or brane theory, these signs must process through the biological vehicle we are given in this lifetime. If we miss these signs, it does not necessarily imply "failure," only a lack of growth. Newton taught us that there is a uniform order in the universe. New science teaches us that everything is connected, whether we're talking about particles (the action), strings (the connection), brane (the theater in which it all plays out), or a combination of the three. Both quantum mechanics and the mystical world deal with the universal unknown—is it such a stretch to think that each is part of the same world, only coming from two entirely different directions? And the force that inhabits them all is pure thought? The scientist is focusing on getting in and the mystic is concentrating on expanding the consciousness outward—yet they are not so different after all! Much like a full moon (an opposition of the sun and the moon equated in our religion to the Lord and Lady), the magickal person who works with science as well as the mind stands in the center—the place of power.

Betwixt and between . . . you straddle the threshold. How do you proceed?

By partaking of the life force of Spirit, the collective soul of humankind grows and prospers. When individuals bow to the blood of hatred, evil acts, pointless hurts, lies, gossip, etc., the soul is weakened and the person enacting this vortex will eventually fall upon his or her own sword. Primal power is not wishing others harm; it is wishing everything right and allowing Spirit to determine what is right and what is needless.

In parts one and two we discussed the importance of cleansing, which keeps negativity from building up within and without, and setting our mental and physical feet upon a spiritual pathway. In this part we are stepping back and viewing the world as a whole, not as a bunch of random, unorchestrated events. We are toiling within our own spiritual garden in an effort to affect the world (as well as ourselves) in a positive way. This is pure science. And this is pure mysticism.

What is done within shows without. And what is done without affects the very fabric of our inner universe. Always.

Indeed, it is highly possible that you are the wormhole of manifestation and how healthy you are in body, mind, and spirit directly relates to your capability of creation. Imagination, then, is not a foolhardy escape from reality but the actual birth mother of the world we live in. If this is so, then belief isn't just a word or a feeling, it is a process.

And if belief is a process?

Then think how much breath we've all wasted on arguing about it, the lives we have lost in the wars over it, and the ridiculous machinations we put ourselves through on a daily basis due to our misconception of it.

If we pay attention to the signs . . . well . . . here is an e-mail from a Black Forest member who received the above information to study prior to the release of this book. It tells you what just might happen if you only pay attention:

one

two

three

four

five

> Signs . . . hmm. It's been an interesting week as far as signs go. I agree with you that it's how we process and interpret them that makes it helpful or not.
>
> I had an incident occur this week that was very instructive on that subject. I was on the way to the gym to work out and as I was getting ready to make the turn into the mall where the gym was, a swallow-type bird started to swoop down into oncoming traffic. I saw it and immediately knew it was going to get hit. I was yelling at it to "Stop! Go back!" but it landed in the road and an oncoming red car struck it dead on. I literally heard the bird "pop" and saw it explode into feathers. It really was dramatic in a gruesome sort of way and upsetting. I made the turn and parked. There was no doubt in my mind that it was a sign. I could tell that by the way I felt. But what on earth did it mean? I had been thinking about our coven's upcoming dedications . . . did it have to do with that? No, didn't feel right. I felt really upset by the incident, felt bad for the bird and almost went home even. I had to ground and center myself before I went in to exercise and decided I would make a conscious effort to pay attention to what was happening around me until I knew what this was about.
>
> When I came out, there was a red work-type van parked directly across from my car. It was around twilight, businesses were closing up, and the parking lot was mostly empty. A man sitting in the van's driver's seat called out, "Excuse me, ma'am," then he mumbled something. I responded with "What?" He mumbled again

and I felt like he wanted me to approach the van. There was no way that was gonna happen because warning bells were going off big time. The third time he mumbled, I just shrugged my shoulders and shook my head and started to get into my car, which was unlocked by this time. He yelled, "Tough IT!" and peeled out of the parking lot at top speed.

Normally I probably would have shrugged it off and went about my business, but because of the bird, I was on the alert and I called my sister when I got home to tell her about it (she belongs to the same gym). It turns out she had a run-in with the same guy the week before and on another day had seen the red van circling the parking lot. I reported him the next day as soon as the place was open (did some mojo too). A police report was filed on him and notices were distributed to all the businesses in the strip mall. Evidently, other women also had run-ins with this dude. I feel like a bad scene was nipped in the bud and the creepy van guy's game is up. The police are on the lookout for him and will be patrolling the area more often around the time he's been known to show up and all the women are on the alert. He's going down.

Who knows how this could have played out if I had interpreted the bird explosion differently or just blown it off as a freaky bird thing? I noticed also that while I was alert, I had made a deliberate choice to plug into positive, harmonious energy before I went in to exercise. I was in the right place at the right time and ready to rock. Another woman might not have been as observant and could have been hurt (it's a women-only gym). Anyway, I thought the whole scenario was interesting and it fits right into what you have been saying about signs, omens, and portents. They are a three-dimensional alert system, almost like an astral guard dog—if you pay attention and learn that the "event" has strings that will lead you to safe choices, you are absolutely ahead of the game.

In this student's experience, the string theory was in play. The blown-up bird (as gross as this may be) was a significant enough three-dimensional event for her to pay attention. Rather than viewing it as a single event, an entity unto itself, she followed the strings that she could not yet readily see, forward and backward. To handle

one

two

three

four

five

the upsetting input, she grounded and centered and, interestingly enough, did a very positive thing: physical exercise. Significantly, she chose to stay alert to determine why the event—this three-dimensional physical manifestation—may have occurred and, in that alert stage, she was able to act in accordance with a harmonious outcome (her protection) and perhaps foiled the perpetration of a future crime too.

Gemstone Spiritual Garden Exercise

Please do not perform this exercise until you have read through all of part three. It is often helpful to students to have hands-on projects to assist them in focusing their energies for magick, meditation, and daily life—this is what the tools in the Craft are used for, such as the wand, the athame, the chalice, etc. Each tool has a collective focus generally agreed upon by most members within the group mind. Some members carry a more detailed analysis of their tools, where others basically see them as a means to an end. Neither interpretation is wrong. The only necessary tool in the Craft, on which all elders seem to agree, is your own true self.

That pencil we talked about earlier is not a separation of those dimensions but a point where all the dimensions come together in a specific energy pattern. This pattern can represent anything: a person, a feeling, a goal, a place, a thing, an animal, etc. Perhaps, as in scientific study, each unfoldment is simply different than the next, yet each influences the other in its own dynamic way—the idea is to harmonize to create. For example, you can call just one quarter in a ritual, but that does not mean that the one you activated doesn't affect the others simply because you focused on the single element (or whatever)—it is all still a part of the circle, still connected to the one.

For this first exercise you will need a sturdy flat box, sand, and a focus (the focus here is creating and building your spiritual garden, although you could use this technique for other applications). Or you are certainly free to clear an outside area in your garden during

one

two

three

four

five

101

one

two

three

four

five

102

Sunburst gemstone illustration.

the warmer months (as I did in my initial experiment), a design that matches your focus and either the gemstones listed or gemstones of your choice with a list of their magickal correspondences. I began this project twenty years into my occult studies, so wherever you may be in your studies, the exercise still applies. The number, type, and size of your gemstones depends directly on your design. Here I used a sunburst of gems with one central piece, but you could use a pentacle, vèvè, seal, or a creation of your own—this is entirely up to you. Choose the design that speaks to you. As this is an exercise of beginnings, timing might be relegated to the new moon, your birthday, a special spiritual day, etc. I used the new moon.

In my original design I chose four types of gemstones: rose quartz, crystal points, amethyst points, and citrine, and used four very large pieces of each gemstone. I chose the crystal points to generate power; the rose quartz for harmony and universal love; the amethyst points for transmuting negative energy, cleansing, protection, and personal empowerment; and the citrine for success. The size of the gemstones depends on what you can procure or how you see the design in your mind's eye.

My central focus was a flowered garden plate with a very large bee—I wanted my spiritual garden to be an active place with industrious energy. To begin, I literally got down on my knees and weeded a medium-sized area in my front yard flower bed. As I pulled the weeds, I concentrated on pulling out the negativity in my life. At the time, an interesting Mercury retrograde, old issues had reared their ugly heads and I was at a loss as to why. I felt that by clearing my spiritual garden and working to the best of my abilities in a positive way I could overcome the noxious energies that appeared to be banging at the closed door.

Note: If you use the box and sand technique, you can perform a cleansing ceremony (as given in previous parts) to reach the same effect. Sand is considered a cleansing agent.

one

two

three

four

five

103

As you work on the cleansing process for your garden, remember that your past actions and decisions bring to you what you are ready for—nothing more, nothing less. This is the same in life as it is in magickal studies. Although you are working with a clean slate to begin (such as the pristine sand or the weeded garden), it is only a level on which to build. What has gone before absolutely affects what you are doing now. You can be given everything and still come out empty-handed if you do not invest in your own spiritual garden—and, I've learned, the more students stress and complain about not having enough material from their teacher, the less likely they will succeed simply because they are ignoring their own creativity. To me, the old "suffer to learn" adage did not mean imposed punishment, but the difficulties and frustrations one encounters when rising to the challenge of learning, and how from that learning unfolds the composite of one's artistic creation. To me, all life is artistry. The suffering artist is not the gaunt, bipolar, starving soul that many people stereotypically picture. The suffering encompasses the mental hurdles you must jump in order to bring thought into form. Whether you are an artist or a mechanic, there is no difference. Screwing in a light bulb in a dark basement ain't easy for anyone! And it will take as long as it takes for each individual person—there is no rushing the process. Like that light bulb in the dark, you can try several times until you manage to line up those threads just right, and even when you do, if someone hits the switch while you are on top of it, you'll be blinded by the light . . . at least momentarily. Those that are permanently blinded due to their own stupidity speak of their "mission" in life ad nauseum—stay away from those people! If someone says, "I'm on a mission . . ."—run!

Now that we have all our supplies, and you believe that your work area is properly prepared, we can move onto the next step: determining the unfoldments of the magick. What do you want to seed in this spiritual garden? For everyone the choices will be different.

one

two

three

four

five

❖

104

I first placed the central piece, a plate, a representation of what I wished to create: the self-mastery of preparing and seeding my own spiritual garden in a positive way, devoid of negativity caused by anger, hurt, insult, or just plain downright stupidity. I envisioned the plate representing the void, the primordial soup from which I could create what I desired. As I did not wish to manifest a physical object, such as a car, I concentrated on the feelings—love, protection, positive change, power, etc.—that might manifest from my own garden and allowed me to experience those emotions in my mind. From there, as I physically set the plate on the ground, I went to "no mind," where all is calm and serene. I stayed there for a while, not mentally meditating but just being still, calm, and relaxed in a communal way with Spirit.

Then I began placing the crystals, empowering each slowly and with purpose from the heart chakra. Moving them out slowly, I placed each of the four crystals at a cardinal point—west, east, north, and then south. Once these were aligned, I chose the rose quartz pieces next, putting them to the right of each crystal, focusing on universal love and empowering them in the same way. I placed the amethyst points to the right of the rose quartz, considering the energies I wanted to cultivate. The working was not to combat negativity alone but to progress to a stage where I could do more positive activities in a spiritual, harmonious way. I empowered the amethyst in the same way for protection and the transmutation of energy. Finally, I added the citrine points, empowered them as well, and placed them beside the amethyst and next to the quartz crystals. As I was doing this I contemplated the infinity sign, the coalescing of energy to produce a positive pattern of spiritual growth from past actions to future empowerment, compacting the dimensions of quantum physics (however many there may be) to a three-dimensional point of manifestation within my own life.

Phase one of the exercise was now complete.

one

two

three

four

five

105

Now . . . I had to live it.

And that is what magick is all about—playing out what you have personally orchestrated and put into place. It is not a guessing game, it is an orderly process. If you have worked on positive, life-affirming applications, then the resulting circumstances may be surprising but harmonious in nature. If you have worked from a negative standpoint, then you will most assuredly reap the culmination of that impetus.

Once the magick for a goal is performed, in an orderly fashion you must live out the resulting pathway, assisted by reading the signs afforded by your own actions. Your will, manifest. When you do the magick you create a blueprint. A pattern. It is as simple (and as complicated) as that. Once I performed the magick, every time a related issue came up, I would go out to that garden and weed it, purposefully throwing out through physical action what I did not desire. The tending of our garden after its initial implementation is just as necessary as the preparation and building process.

And this is where many students fall short of the mark. They do the magick, but they are uncertain of how to handle the consequences, as magick is not linear—it is of its own nature, which is that of quantum physics, carrying its own signs and portents (as Lady Shantih showed us). We must learn to read what is given to us by our own acts of energy manifestation. This is not as easy as we would like and is far beyond the basic contemplation of Wicca, which is a philosophy as much as it is a modern religion.

Playing Out the Magick

Learning how to handle what you have created is just as difficult as learning how to manifest what you desire. So many times students do the magick and then are confounded when things occur that they didn't expect, especially for difficult situations or amorphous requests (such as peace, harmony, enlightenment, etc.). This is

one
two
three
four
five

106

a three-dimensional world. All magick is an act of balance. If your three-dimensional world is in the toilet, then it is a guarantee that situations are probably going to get worse before they get better, so that balance can occur. How you initially worded your spell and the thoughts and visualizations you created with that mystery energy of thought are vitally important when cultivating the event or item you wish to procure, allowing you to control what you receive and how it comes to you. That's why we have those sayings: "Don't call up what you can't put down." And "Be careful what you ask for—you just might get it." Granted, a minimum of specifics can get you what you want faster, but it can also unfold a compendium of loose ends that weren't necessary and are sometimes downright difficult to deal with. For example, "I want all my bills paid by the thirtieth of this month" might bring you trials and tribulations you never thought possible. Yeah, the bills got paid, but what the heck did you have to suffer with for six months past that? Even if you did keep your spiritual and personal life relatively in order, who is to say that a past decision made months ago that you forgot about, deeming it trivial, won't explode like a wild card right under your nose?

Yes, magick is for everyone because anyone can inherently perform it (whether they know they are doing it or not—it is a natural function of all human beings because its premise lies in quantum physics); however, the mystery lies in the recognition and proper application of its power before (cleansing), during (the performance), and after (how you handle the outcome), not in the fact that it exists or not. All three steps—before, during, and after—make up the entirety of the application and without monitoring all three, stuff can happen that you didn't intend. For the skilled practitioner, the question should not be "What will happen if . . . "—the statement should be "This will happen now." Looking at it differently may jam your finger in a light socket twenty times over! This is why occult teachers are so adamant on particular elements, especially

one
two
three
four
five

107

one

two

three

four

five

❖

108

those predicated on their own experiences, such as cleansing, casting the circle, being specific in your requests, remembering to finish magickally what you've begun, sealing applications, etc. If you don't do these things, then you are simply asking for difficulties. Drilling such steps into the head of the student isn't easy, and some simply never learn. And, even though you've gone over all these things a hundred times with a particular student, a jerk is a jerk is a jerk, meaning they can have all the magickal keys and jingle them frantically in your face when they are displeased at a decision you've made on their training (or even expulsion), but if their behavior is spiritually inhibited (lies, boasting, gossip, stealing, destruction of property, megalomania) then, frankly, it's like spitting in the wind. Eventually Spirit (not you) will take away all those magickal keys and each door will slam shut, door by door by door, in their faces. This is an incredibly painful process for these people. Spirit does take away ability. Karma is a bitch.

How do you properly play out your magick? By remembering the pencil explanation: You only see what condenses at the point of entry, and you must also be aware that energy lies at each end of the stick that you cannot see, but of which you can be cognizant. This energy brings signs, omens, and portents into your life as your desire (or even nonmagickal events and issues) unfolds in your three-dimensional world. Awareness opens the first lock, acknowledgment releases the second. Do not forget, too, that a three-dimensional object is constantly moving of its own accord—it is only stable because the collective unconscious says it is stable, thereby allowing it to be in this world. (Yes, I know, you could go all over the map with this one.) As the volleys of the results of your desires reach you, you can learn to swing your racket of action in a positive, solution-oriented way, scoring points rather than suffering a black eye. Understanding that what is entering your life may be a direct result of a magickal application (even if the two don't seem to match at first) broadens your future expertise.

Eleven Mysteries Exercise

For this application you will need a quartz crystal (a good clear one with a point works well); your specific, focused desire written on a piece of parchment paper (add sigils if you like); your two hands; and a strip of flat paper forty-three inches long and at least two inches wide. Beginning at the right end, mark off two-inch increments with a ruler until you have nine marks on the paper. Do the same thing with the left side of the paper. Once you have read this exercise through, feel free to decorate the paper as you see fit in accordance with your own creativity on the technique. Before you actually perform the exercise, practice the charm, which is in French and English, so that your first application will have a smoother performance. The purpose of using two languages is to force the brain to switch gears while manifesting energy. The soft, musical French adds mystery to the working as well.

one

two

three

four

five

109

When you are ready to work the spell, have chosen your timing, and ironed out the kinks of being specific, gathered your tools and feel ready to rock 'n roll, lay the long paper out on a smooth surface. Place your petition in the center of the paper, at the open space that is bracketed by the marks you made previously. Put the crystal on top of the petition. Set a white or colored candle that reflects your intention above the petition (but off the paper). Turn out the lights; this one works well for the first time in total darkness.

Take a deep breath. Ground and center. Light the candle, saying, "From out of the darkness and into the light, the focus is pure, the manifestation is right." This statement means that you are casting the circle with the aura of the flame and that only positive results can be achieved by the spell. Read that again so you know what you are saying when you are saying it.

There are two ways to proceed: you can either move your hands from the center of the paper out or from the outside of the paper in. We're working from the outer edges to the crystal in this example, thinking of that pencil analogy—from energy to solidification in the three-dimensional world. If you are trying to materialize an object, place a lodestone or pair of lodestones beside the crystal.

Take another deep breath. Place your hands, palms down, one on each side of the paper. Find "no mind" within yourself. Slowly open your hands so that they still rest on the table, but the palms are facing each other—still the same distance apart—one on each end of the paper. As you say the Mystery Chant, bring your hands together—a mark at a time. This means that you will be saying the chant eleven times in all, while focusing on the crystal in the middle that rests upon your desire. Begin with the first ten repetitions.

one

two

three

four

five

110

> *"Venez à moi.* (pause) *Come to me.*
>
> *Déplier.* (pause) *Unfold.*
>
> *Dimension to dimension.*
>
> [move your hands in to the next line]
>
> *Déplier.* (pause) *Unfold."*
>
> (repeat charm)

As you utter the charm, your hands will most likely grow significantly warm and you may feel as if you are actually holding something—which, in essence, you are. If you are focusing on drawing a material object, visualize that object in the center, above the crystal, as much as possible.

The eleventh repetition is the final one. And as you utter this portion, close your hands around the crystal and close your eyes, feeling the power surge between your hands. As you utter the last word ("Déplier!"), with a rush of breath, open your eyes and look immediately up to the right—that place where we manufacture from fantasy into reality of the spoken word—and say, "Cachet! Tow!" which means "hide the spell" (yes, I know that's not exactly how it translates, but this is the spell). You may also add, "May this spell not reverse, or place upon me any curse" or any other definitive statement to ensure a positive manifestation. Carry the paper with you until your desire manifests. Burn the paper, cleanse the crystal, and thank the gods when you are satisfied with the results.

Variations on this exercise (and worth experimentation) include the following:

- Working from the center, holding the crystal, and moving your hands outward.

- Drawing a large infinity sign on the table, with the crystal in the center.

- Lining up candles and lighting them, from one end to the other to represent the eleven dimensions.

- Once you have learned the cadence with the eleven repetition, lose the paper.

- Make the paper a wooden form if you teach a high number of students and wish to explain this technique or quantum physics in general.

- Tape the infinity symbol (or a symbol of your choice) on top of your drum and drum the spell.

one

two

three

four

five

111

Weeding Your Garden

Once your spiritual garden is in place and you continue to work through a series of positive, growth-oriented issues, there will be a time or two when you will need to weed out any negativity that may have managed to sneak in there. Fear is a big fat weed that spreads quickly and is so pervasive that we don't often realize that it has gotten out of hand. Magickal training will bring our fears to light in order to cut them from us, as it is extremely well put in the following piece; yet, unlike those who succumb to it, this powerful Witch was determined to weed her spiritual garden of this nasty pest. With her second elevation in a traditional Wiccan format less than a month away, this student of the occult began to enter her

own ritual of descent, very much associated with most second elevation ceremonies in the Craft. In the descent one must face their
own fears, cast off old and crusty habits that do not serve them, and
gather power to rise above one's own orchestrated complications.
The second level is all about dealing with the self and gaining the
mastery needed to continue on one's spiritual path.

one

two

three

four

five

112

Dear _____,

For the past few days I have made myself take a ruthless and
honest inventory of myself and my state of mind. What I found
with the help of Spirit is that since this past February I have been
living with an incredible amount of fear that has colored my
every thought, action, reaction, and attitude. My fears have been
many . . . the fear of "not enough" (material world), the fear of
disappointing those I love, the fear of discovery—that someone
will find out that I'm a fake and "not good enough," fear of myself and my own power and abilities, the fear of losing the core of
"me" in this journey through my studies (I believe this is called
"ego death" and it is by far the scariest of the fears listed) . . . there
are more, but they are basically offshoots of the ones listed above.
These have ultimately culminated in the pervasive fear and anxi-
ety that I am in danger, that I am going to be hurt. This has also
(not surprisingly) manifested in some health issues, not serious,
but wakeup calls that I cannot continue living under this self-imposed stress level.

I have decided that something has to give or I will simply im-
plode, so this is what I have come up with—my personal game
plan. I'm telling you this because it's only fair that you know
what's going on.

1. Use my words positively to manifest the positive.

2. Do not take anything personally. (This one will be very
hard. I played around with this one—what could I take personally
and what could I not. Spirit was/is pretty definite on "nothing."
Nothing can be taken personally because each person is living
their own "truth" . . . their truth has nothing to do with mine and
therefore, nothing anyone says or does "to" me can be taken personally.)

3. Nothing can hurt me. (The energy I'm feeling is not about me [see above]. I can acknowledge it and let it pass by, or I can choose to not open myself to it at all. It's my reality, my "illusion" . . . I can control what comes in and out and how I respond to it.)

4. Do my best at all times, no more, no less. (If I've done my best on whatever task I'm on than I cannot beat myself up. I've done the best I can do, I've given it my full effort and that's it. No judge/victim roleplaying will be acceptable within myself.)

5. Stay in the moment. (Now is all I have. Enjoy it. In my meditations I was given the thought of the Angel of Death. This angel sweeps up all that has been, providing for the Now. He does not make any promises for the future. His gift is the present moment only. If I remember this I think it will be easier to stay in the Now . . . it's all I am guaranteed.)

6. There is nothing wrong with power, but there is something wrong with refusing to acknowledge it. (Spirit showed me everything has power. The pine tree contains immense power and uses it for its own well-being, which in turn benefits everything in its environment. I must begin to discipline myself to harness my power for my own benefit and well-being which will in turn benefit those around me. I had been going about this bass-ackwards, BTW).

7. Fear is a way to avoid change. Change cannot be avoided. (Oh, what a rub! But the fear I have been feeling is all about the "me" I have been told to be by outside sources and early conditioning. I chose to believe these things and now that "me" is a parasite and is not willing to go easily. It is a many-headed monster that has thrown fear into my psyche whenever it feels threatened. This is how I describe the ego death. There is the true me in there and it is stronger than the parasite. I have chosen to do away with the false me. Spirit showed the way—stop fighting, stop fearing, All Is Well.)

8. Refrain, don't repress (emotions).

So, there it is. Forty-eight hours of digging at my wounds. I feel better . . .

I am a realist, though; I will fall on my face with a few of these a few times. I am a creature of habit and I have habituated myself to these negative thoughtforms and behaviors. But I think I may actually come out on the other side of this.

one

two

three

four

five

113

The references I used to make my list are as follows:

The Four Agreements: A Toltec Wisdom Book by Don Miguel Ruiz

Conversations with God (1, 2, & 3) by Neale Donald Walsch

Illusions by Richard Bach

A Woman's Way Through the Twelve Steps by Stephanie S. Covington, Ph.D.

The Hiding Place by Corrie Ten Boom with John and Elizabeth Sherrill

My own writings in my burgeoning Pagan Recovery Program—Healer, heal thyself! smirk >:)

one

two

three

four

five

114

Let Spirit Show the Way

Ever feel totally overwhelmed? Like you've just got so much to do and so little time to do it? Have you ever sat just staring at something, your brain frozen because you simply don't know what to do first? Here's a simple technique to "git 'er done"!

Supplies: Paper, pencil, rolled quartz gemstones, amethyst (at least one piece), white candle, your choice of power/activity magickal oil, and scissors.

Write down on a piece of paper all those things you have to do. Don't worry about prioritizing, the magick and your mind are going to do that for you effortlessly! Just make the list. For as many items on the list, choose an equal number of rolled quartz gemstones. Place these in a black bag along with your priority list. Shake lightly, then spill the stones on a soft cloth. Do not shake out the list. Do not touch the stone pattern. Remove the list from the bag and cut it into slips, one item per slip of paper. Place the slips of paper in the bag. Empower the bag and the stone pattern for ease in action and accomplishment. Now, pull one slip of paper from the bag and place it on top of the stone pattern. Do the task on the paper. When the task is finished, burn the slip of paper and wash the stone in running water. Dry. Place the stone in the bag with the other slips. This is to give you power and momentum to complete the other tasks. Repeat taking out one piece of paper from the bag, finishing the task, burning the paper, cleansing the stone and returning it to the bag until the pattern of activity is gone and all the rolled crystals are back in the bag. Wash the amethyst, dry, and return it to the black bag. Now the bag is ready for the next time that you feel you have too much to do and too little time to accomplish what is required!

Cosmograph for Spiritual Power

Many magickal people enjoy working with designs for talismans and sigils. Unless you create it yourself, however, you may not know all the nuances, especially if the design is older and there is no way to speak to the original creator. What may have been taught about a design a hundred years ago could have a totally new twist by the time someone hands it to you. I created the Cosmograph for Spiritual Power—a line art design—that incorporates numerous occult principles focused on the enlightenment of self specifically for this section. I chose line art to keep the design simple and easy to re-create, purposefully staying away from the more familiar symbols of moons, stars, pentacles, etc., in an effort to incorporate sacred geometry.

The center of this design is the Spirit Circle—a sacred vortex representing the four elemental directions and the point of manifestation. Write your desire in or on the back of the circle when re-creating the drawing, if you like. The four diamonds stand for the occult principle "as above, so below" and the necessity to unfold energy through all the dimensions (however many that may be) to create your desire (in this case, spiritual empowerment). The four wings are stylized representations of feathers or leaves, used in ancient times to sweep out a ritual space. I chose four so that you can envision them sweeping around the design in a clockwise motion, clearing out any negativity in a positive way. The stars on the end of the feathers (and elsewhere in the design) are stylized and look like big asterisks. These are portals where energy can move in and out of the

one

two

three

four

five

115

one

two

three

four

five

❖

116

The Cosmograph for Spiritual Power.

design. They represent day and night, the sun and the moon, balance, mastery, and movement. There are ten stars in this design—which factors to one—the totality of the whole. Energies must become one to create a particular pattern. The triangles capped with horns are power points incorporating manifestation through the three known dimensions, and the hook at the end is to draw in and capture the energy. The *S* shape at the top of the design is a stylized version of the infinity symbol. The stairs represent the building process that it takes to become a better person—it doesn't happen overnight, and is a reminder that we should always try to move onward and upward, making decisions to empower rather than succumb to lower levels of behavior. The first stair level contains eleven dots, speaking of self-mastery. The second level contains seven dots, a magickal number of victory and movement, and the last tier contains three dots—the representation of spirituality, three-dimensional change, and earth, sea, and sky. The steps are connected to the design to keep the energy moving yet provide a solid base from which you can always draw. Too, the stairs speak of your ability to analyze and the power of your thought. The boxes speak of how we compartmentalize thoughts, shift them into a pattern without boundaries, then relegate them again into something different, with new lines of delineation. Finally, the dots on the upper portion of the design, of which there are six, ties into alchemical formulary.

The design can be activated in one of two ways: Use a rattle to sound out the design or draw a pentacle in the air over the central portion of the drawing. If using candle magick, place four candles, one at each power point (triangle and horns), to draw in the energy to the center of the design, which represents your petition or what you desire to manifest. Any herbs, gems, stones, etc., should be placed on the stars (as many or as few as you like).

You can draw the design on paper and place it in a poppet, gris-gris bag, dream pillow, etc., or make a larger design directly on

one
two
three
four
five

117

one

two

three

four

five

118

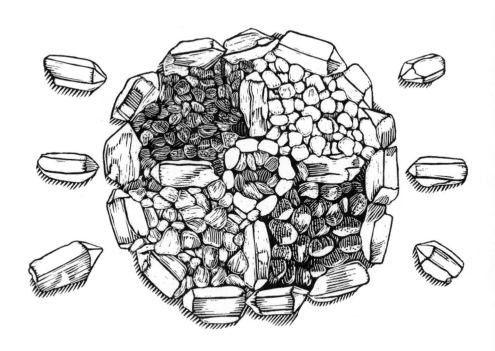

*Stone mandala built with crystals, sugalite, rose quartz,
amethyst, sodalite, and blue lace agates.*

your personal altar and work with it for eleven days (for self-mastery). Use your creativity to enhance the sigil by weaving your own abilities of enchantment to lift the spirit and manifest more desirable behaviors in your self.

A Light in the Garden: Forever Healing Flame

Originally designed as an outdoor project for an AIDS patient healing ritual, you can re-create this exercise in your home; however, you will need an area that can remain undisturbed and the flame must be monitored at all times. The instructions here will give you a stone mandala that is approximately fifteen inches in diameter. To make a smaller one, cut the number of stones in half. You will need one pound rolled rose quartz crystals; one pound rolled sodalite gemstones; one pound rolled amethyst gemstones; one pound blue lace agate gemstones; ¼ pound sugalite gemstones; 21–26 large quartz points; ¼ pound rolled crystal quartz; one flat piece of flagstone, about 8 x 8 inches or 6 x 6 inches; a drill with a drill bit for stone; two wicks (cotton for indoors, synthetic for outdoors); smokeless lamp oil; and a stainless steel bowl (you can use glass, but if you are doing this for an outside ritual, especially in the fall or winter, the heat-safe glass can crack with the temperature fluctuations).

one

two

three

four

five

119

Although designed specifically for AIDS patients, the mandala can be used for other healings as well. The circle ring, constructed using large crystal points from Brazil, collects and activates the healing energy. Six different gemstone types are used for self-actualization and alchemical change. As above, so below.

The center of the circle contains sugalite from South Africa—the "love" stone representing spiritual transformation. The stone is thought to promote positive thoughts, protect one from shock or disappointment, and has been used by magickal people for cancer patients. Rose quartz (up and to the right) is for empowerment through love and kindness. It's a stone of compassion and healing used in all manner of magick for those who have fallen ill. The stones in the lower right are amethyst from South Africa, the gem of transformation, healing, and protection. The upper right contains sodalite from Burma, encouraging a calm mind and emotional balance as well as cleansing the organs and the immune system. Lower left pictures blue lace agate, promoting peace, spirituality, and balancing the chakras.

Take your time creating your stone mandala, focusing on what you wish to bring forth into this dimension. A black and white illustration does not give this design justice, but it will show you how I built the one here.

When the design is completed, empower under both the sun and the moon when each is at its zenith—therefore, you will be working with the design twice to activate it.

The Forever Light (which isn't really forever, just a symbol of an unending light) is very easy to put together. Drill two holes in the flagstone about an inch and a half apart. Partially fill the small stainless steel bowl with lamp oil (smokeless is best). Don't overfill or you'll have a mess and create a fire hazard. Carefully set the bowl on the design. If it wobbles, make adjustments—it is okay to move the stones because you've already done the activation of the pattern. Carefully set the flagstone "cover" on top of the bowl. Thread the wicks into the holes you have drilled, leaving only a bit of wick above the surface of the stone. Give the wicks several minutes to soak up the lamp oil.

The ritual is very simple. Cast a circle and call the quarters. Sit in front of the design and meditate on the healing you wish to provide and to whom, then light the wicks. While you watch the flame, meditate, drum, or chant, raising power. When the hair on your arms starts to tingle or you feel the gathering of energy (it feels like you are a cat, ready to pounce), let the energy flow over the design and up by moving your arms over the design and up. The work for this day is done. You can allow the flame to continue to burn (closely

one

two

three

four

five

120

monitored) or extinguish the flame. Trim the wick before using it again. Warning: Because the flagstone cap only sits on the bowl without a proper lid, be very, very careful of children, pets, and ritual participants. It is best to position the mandala and the flame where no one can bump into it, even by accident.

Summary

one

two

three

four

five

121

This part contained only two main exercises and a great deal of dissertation and theory on science and the occult. Its main purpose was not to inform you "what is," but to stretch your mind to "what could be." My focus was to encourage you to look outside of the box (or the book) and acknowledge that the world is full of mysteries to contemplate and, in that quiet analysis, to determine what may or may not be true for you. Learning to work within the confines of a structure (Craft teachings) and drawing in information gathered by the self (the study of quantum physics, accurate historical research, or through one's own trial and error, etc.) is no easy task. It requires guts. Even if I am inaccurate on my postulations of science and magick, you hopefully have learned these things:

One, what we call "magick" is natural phenomena and not relegated to special people.

Two, it takes courage to acknowledge our own idiosyncrasies, let alone examine them and then alter what we feel does not serve us well in an ever-changing world and still keep up with the partner, the job, the kids, the dog, and whatever else.

Three, we have far more power than we realize.

Four, indeed, our world is a mystery.

If you are using this book as a training vehicle, there is enough material here to keep you busy from moon to moon and beyond. You cannot build your spiritual garden in one day, although you can make a conscious effort to begin anew at any given moment. As the quote at the beginning of the part states, cultivating your own inner garden will most likely occur in a series of mental shifting of gears. A personal journal or even a series of short crib notes may be extremely helpful as you work through this stage of your development. Each movement forward in contemplation will bring new ideas, challenges, and spiritual work to do. You can ignore this work or you can embrace it.

one

two

three

four

five

FOUR

As Above, So Below

The excitement at the dinner table filled our corner of the restaurant with palpable enthusiasm. Our daughter was finally home from a fourteen-month armed service overseas tour; as we celebrated having her safely with us, the topic of conversation turned to magick, science, music, human behavior, signs, omens, and the construction of this book. The age range of our guests spanned from seventeen to seventy-eight years, and several had never, ever sat with a magickal family before, let alone heard the myriad of topics bouncing over the top of steak, seafood, and salad, and me waving a steak knife at the height of my dissertation of magick and the quantum world. It was not that I had discovered something new—but that I was *myself* perceiving things differently. At my enthusiasm, my daughter smiled and said, "Mother, please put the knife down. You're scaring people." Hmm . . . no wonder our waitress didn't seem to be anywhere about. Humor ran high at her statement with numerous giggles and a loud guffaw or two, and the conversation continued with gusto!

Mixing magick, the real world (whatever that may be), and spirituality together is not an easy task for anyone. Every individual who tries to brew these three volatile states together will have their own unique hurdles to overcome. The restaurant scene is a prime example of how juggling disparate yet possibly synchronistic energies applies to everyday life—in this instance, time, place, present, experience, people, emotions, learning, science, love, magick, knowledge, and focus can actually create a fun-filled, harmonious moment even with that ubiquitous observer (the waitress) to enliven the pot. The table, devoid of the human presence, could not have created it.

In the first three parts (or lessons), we covered preparation, the journey, and the partnership of science and magick through a spiritual pathway, culminating in exercises and discussions on cultivating your spiritual garden. In this lesson we move from the raised beds of the astral to the earthly bed of Mother Nature. By learning to mix her bounty in a spiritual way through physical practice, we embrace our abilities to manifest our desires. Since herbal tables and information can be a bit boring, I chose instead to fertilize your interest with a lesson on magickal powders and herbal blends.

Unveiling the Mystery of Magickal Powders and Herbal Blends

An herbal blend is usually a high-quality mix of herbs chosen for their color, magickal properties, scent, and texture that sometimes contains fragrance or essential additives. These blends are used directly as offerings to the gods, in gris-gris bags, to stuff poppets and dream pillows, for enchanted potpourri, as a centerpiece decoration in ritual, or scattered around empowered candles. A magickal powder is a ground herbal formula that often contains essential oil blends and other additives that are not necessarily natural, and it is used to activate items or energies in spellwork and ritual. As the formulation of each is extremely close in detail, we'll cover the intricacies of the powder with the understanding that the technique of creating each is much the same, although powder instructions are more detailed.

Magickal Powders
Research into magickal powders uncovers a compendium of recipes that differ from area to area, state to state, and country to country. In-

one
two
three
four
five

126

gredients are also influenced by individual teachers and practitioners as they learn and grow in their chosen craft. In quality powders, scent is a factor for both magickal correspondences as well as aromatic purposes, which we'll cover a little further on. Although magickal powders are not commonly found in New Age stores (other than the occasional Fairy Dust or Angel Powder, which is usually body glitter) or modern Wiccan practices, you will find them in Witchcraft grimoires (Herman Slater was a great proponent of powders and handmade incense) as well as much older material. They are extremely popular in Voudon and Santeria (which are religions) and Hoodoo (which is a magickal system vast in its array of practitioners).

There are basically three types of magickal powders:

one

two

three

four

five

- Those with a fine base talc, sometimes colored. If not made by yourself, these mass-produced formulas contain little herb and a lot of talc. You also have no clue how old it is, which is an important factor in magick, or who made it.

- Those that include finely ground powders from an herbal supplier. The drawback here, as with the one above, is that very fine powder is not lung friendly, but—more important in magickal work—you have no idea what you are getting. From my experience, these powders have not retained their scent or texture: important factors in magickal herbal work. And, too, as with the first type of powder, you have no idea how old the powder is when you receive it.

- The third category of powder is handground, which is therefore coarser in nature, retains its scent, and you know exactly what you put in there. These powders are prepared with a mortar and pestle, though some magickal practitioners grind the largest pieces with a coffee grinder and then use a mortar and pestle to finish the magick, as the hand movement and the chanting does much to enhance the powder. If color is desired, diamond glitter (used in soap-making products and gel candles) can add that "flash of Spirit" and merge with your color correspondence rather than colored talc (which is fairly messy). The practical rule here is to put color in powders you don't care who sees and keep color or glitter out of those powders that will be used in public. This third category, usually made personally by the magickal practitioner also contains a variety of unnatural or unusual elements (see "additives" on page 130).

one

two

three

four

five

✵

·

Of the three, magickally speaking, the last type of powder is considered the most powerful of the enchanted formulas. The choice to use a magickal powder is an extremely economical one. Powders cost less to make, do not waste our natural resources, are easy to store, simple to use, can be mixed easily with many magickal practices, and lend well to secrecy, which is a high priority if you are looking at magick as a science governed by quantum physics—the less observers, the better! As great quantities of herb are not needed by the practitioner, when shopping for ingredients one can choose the higher-priced organics, which usually carry a better scent and are of better quality. Too, making magickal powders can be a fun lesson in teaching students because not only is the student able to take something home with them, they learn quickly the properties and correspondences of the herbs, can grasp the importance of the ceremony chosen, and can experience a wide range of magickal techniques in creating one simple formula, culminating in the spiritual lesson "as above, so below." Most importantly, students learn that the powder is an alchemical pattern in itself that can be enhanced by the spiritual practices used in its creation and become a powerhouse in their personal magick.

Basic Supplies for Magickal Powders

GLASS BOWLS for mixing (metal is thought to magickally taint the powder). You will need at least two—one for the raw herb mixture and one for the finished powder. Clear bowls work well because you can see what you are doing through the entire process.

WOODEN SPOONS. Some practitioners use special spoons hand-carved with magickal sigils.

MORTAR AND PESTLE. The size depends on the number of ingredients and how large a batch you choose to make.

MALLET for crushing raw resins such as frankincense, myrrh, and dragon's blood, as well as some of the tougher roots: Solomon's seal, angelica, etc.

ESSENTIAL OILS. Only 2–3 drops are used for small batches of powder (12–14 for larger batches); be careful of overpowering the natural aroma of the blend. The oil can be added to the raw herb mixture or massaged in with the fingers when the grinding process is completed. If a particular ingredient is not available in herbal form, many times an essential oil may be added in minute amounts. Not only does this round out the magickal pattern of the formula, the oil also heightens the aromatic properties of the mixture, which can affect the performance of the practitioner in positive ways. As a result many current blends contain both herbals and oils in an effort to capture the totality of magickal essence.

MEASURING SPOONS.

BOLLINE. This is a magickal knife designed specifically for cutting herbs.

one

two

three

four

five

129

SAFETY MASK. Myrrh, especially, can cause lung problems and many of the powders emit dust while grinding.

RAW HERBS of your choice.

ADDITIVES such as ground gems, stones, feathers, shells, and bones; ashes of a petition or photo, graveyard dirt, saltpeter (careful, this is highly flammable), iron dust, rust, and glitter; shredded and pulverized paper money, newsprint, pictures of saints, parchment talismans, rune stones, and tarot cards; dirt from a bank, a jail, a successful corporation, your job, or the property of someone who has been trying to hurt you; scrapings from a car, gravestone, church, or statuary—the list is almost endless. Basically, if you can get it small enough, it can go in the powder!

STORAGE. Although glass jars are best for storage, heavy plastic can be used. The shelf life of a magickal powder is approximately six months in glass and four in plastic, or a year if you use a food sealer.

Choosing Your Ingredients

The number of ingredients in any magickal powder varies—however, a good recipe is thought to measure the totality of the whole, always factoring to "one." Much like the Eye of Horus, which is an ancient Egyptian mathematical formula for measuring parts of herbs, so, too, the magickal powder is also a numeric pattern that should always equal one of the measurements (dry or liquid). For example, if you used eight herbs, you may wish to use eight ⅛ teaspoons of each herb, thus equaling 8/8 or one whole; or, if you wish to follow the older formulas, seven ⅛ teaspoons of seven herbs with the last ⅛ dedicated to Spirit, which could be an unusual ingredient such as ashes or powdered stone.

one
two
three
four
five

130

Powders, like perfumes and essential magickal oils, are sometimes mixed by "notes"—taking the language from music, which is also mathematical in nature and therefore a numeric matrix and a series of magickal patterns in its own right. Powders and oils blended in this manner include base notes, heart notes, and top notes. This type of formulation separates the spellwork into three different areas, much like the function of the zodiac signs, where the base of the formula is like the fixed signs—a platform that holds the matrix together and gives a primary undercurrent of strength both in magick and in scent. The base note speaks of the main magickal desire (love, money, health, happiness, protection, exorcism, etc.), the heart note is the energy spark that motivates the powder (the cardinal signs of the zodiac), and the top note is the blending agent that holds the formula together, much like the mutable signs. The analogy of powders and perfumery is not complete, as essential oils do react differently (scent wise) in overall formulary than powders, and what might be considered a heart note in perfumery/essential oil blending may very well be a base note in magickal powders.

one

two

three

four

five

131

The base notes of the powder are the aromatic drumbeat of the mixture and often carry the fixative properties of the formula. They are not necessarily the largest portion of the mixture because many can totally overpower the entire design. This part of the powder is often strong and full-bodied. As in perfumery (but not exactly like it), base notes in powders include many of the magickal woods and bark (sandalwood, cedar, pine, bergamot); the resins (frankincense, copal, dragon's blood); roots such as orris; highly aromatic leaves such as bay, patchouli, lavender, and white ceremonial sage; and beans (tonka beans have a strong vanilla aroma [be careful, they are considered poisonous] and of course the vanilla bean [the price of which has gone far out of sensibility]). As with all ingredients in any enchanted powder, much of the base magickally corresponds to a specific intent, such as banishment, exorcism, drawing love and friends, money, success, happiness, healing, etc. One or more base notes can be chosen—the number is up to the practitioner.

The heart note in a powder (sometimes called middle notes or Coeur notes in perfumery) specifically concentrates on the movement of the formula. This part of the recipe can be associated with the cardinal signs, the signs of activation and new beginnings, and therefore is fine-tuned to the specific function of the powder as well as its capability of energy activation. These herbs include cinnamon, vervain, galangal, ginger, cypress, black pepper, red pepper, some florals, clove, nutmeg, geranium, etc. Fire element herbs are often the most popular if it is felt a great deal of power is needed; air is second.

The top note of the powder is the blending agent. It ensures that all magickal correspondences work smoothly together. Basil is a major favorite here; also lemon, orange, mint, chamomile, rosemary, juniper berry, myrrh resin, and benzoin. Again, much like perfumery, but not exactly the same.

The deity or spirits served during the process of making a magickal powder are also important to the overall construction of the formula. In Afro-Caribbean structures (Voodoo and Santeria), the ingredients used are considered to be owned by the spirits and have no planetary associations at all (though again, the knowledge of the practitioner can negate this statement). The herbs are categorized as sweet or bitter, which have nothing to do with taste but rather with the properties and characteristics of the plant. The bitter herbs are used to remove evil, negativity, bad luck, etc., where the sweet herbs bring in the money, prosperity, love, luck, health, etc. Yet, in the European mixtures,[1] the planetary associations of the plant replace the cultural spirits and taboos of the Afro-Caribbean counterparts.

one
two
three
four
five

❖

132

---

1. For example, where German Americana met head-on with Southern folklore—a form of Hoodoo found commonly in West Virginia and southern Pennsylvania, next to the Appalachian Mountains.

Some practitioners also add an additional herbal fixative to the powder (over the base note to ensure longevity), such as ground orris root (iris root), which strengthens the aromatic properties of the herbs and holds the essential oils (if used). Oak moss has much the same function.

Preparation

The more spiritually enhanced the environment in which the powder is prepared (type of ceremony chosen, cleanliness of materials, the absence of negative people, etc.), the more likely the powder will function at its full magickal capacity. I've learned that from the moment the grinding and mixing process has begun, the powder reacts better later if you move into the alpha state through chanting or whispering magick. Again, the ceremony involved in the creation of the magickal powder depends upon the practitioner and can be highly specialized based upon their magico-religious beliefs, cultural background, and prior training.

A powder is considered "good" if it is handground with a mortar and pestle in a ritual environment according to the signs and the phase of the moon. Powders to draw things toward you should be mixed at the new and waxing moons. Powders for banishment and protection should be ground during the waxing moon. Powders for exorcism should be prepared during the dark of the moon. This is fairly standard with just about every occult teaching; however, the moon in the signs actually has just as much influence (or more, depending on how into astrology your teacher may be) on the overall formula. Quick tips? Here goes!

ARIES: Beginnings, attack, and new experiences—the true pioneer. (Cardinal)

TAURUS: Stability, investment, and long-term effects on things you value. (Fixed? Boy, is it ever!)

one

two

three

four

five

133

one

two

three

four

five

134

GEMINI: Movement and intelligence (but not necessarily wisdom), communication. (Mutable)

CANCER: Emotional issues, psychism to some degree and the "roots" of an issue; women's mysteries, moon magick, and things that are associated with your legacy. (Cardinal)

LEO: Loyalty, children, talent, and gambling. (No kidding, Leos may be "fixed"—but true Leos are very good at "chance.")

VIRGO: Analysis, solutions, stealth magick, occult mastery, and animal magick. (Mutable, but they are cold and calculating, no doubt about it.)

LIBRA: Artistic, socialization (on a lighter scale), and partnership magick. (Just be careful: a true Libra can't make a choice to save their soul because they want to be fair at all costs.) (Cardinal)

SCORPIO: Perfect for investigation, general occult, sex, death, and other people's money. (Fixed)

SAGITTARIUS: Legal issues, foreign affairs, publishing, and—no kidding—one-night stands. (Mutable)

CAPRICORN: Business, entrepreneurship, investment, authority, and dealing with older people and "rules." (Cardinal)

Those individuals who are well-traveled or cross-trained in several magickal faiths tend to add a wide spectrum of variety in herbals, oils, and instructions relating to the grinding, conjuring, and use of magickal powders, and may perform one type of ceremony for a particular type of powder and a completely different ceremony for another. You can tell the length and breadth of an individual's herbal/

powders training by the variety of herbals used in their formulas. Although recipes and instructions for use are sometimes freely given, the activation procedures at the creation of the vehicle are held under a thick cloak of mystique—considered near and dear to the heart of the practitioner. Chants, charms, songs, or dances intricate to the creation are not usually shared with the general public. This could be due to oaths taken at the onset of the learning environment or responsibilities previously agreed upon in a magickal religion or order. The activation by the creator is only half of the magick; the true magick lies within the individual who utilizes the powder.

Feeding the Powder

It is believed that powders, like other magickal vehicles, such as rune stones, sigils, and vèvès, must be "fed" to be activated. Feeding is commonly done in liquid form, with white rum as the most popular, followed by bourbon, perfume (brands differ between Voudon Santeria, and Wicca), sometimes White Lightening (which is a grain alcohol once popular in Appalachia), magickal sprays (a combination of vodka or perfumer's alcohol, distilled water, essential oils, and an emulsifier, which allows the oil to bond with the liquid formula), and finally spring water, although other substances are known to be used for specific recipes, such as perishable floral waters. The liquid is sprayed onto the powder at least three times, sometimes seven, eight, or nine times, depending upon the original purpose of the powder. When a powder is "fed" also differs. Some magickal workers feed their powders as a last step in the ceremonial process before the powder is actually used in magick or handed over to the client, friend, or circle member. Others believe that the person who actually does the magickal application is responsible for feeding the formula, thereby bonding their energy (their desire) to the powder so that it can work at its fullest potential. You may wish to use the magickal powder conjuration, written below, when activating your formula.

one

two

three

four

five

135

Magickal Powder Conjuration

This very simple conjuration invokes the mindset of "as above, so below," the power of one standing between the cycle of the moon and sun as they travel across the heavens and therefore create a magick circle around the earth, the premise of bringing equally opposing energies together to work in tandem, the idea of a quantum physics pattern in the spoken word, the rippling flow of all energy, and the affirmation (faith or belief) that the practitioner is knowledgeable and filled with the power to change.

> *"Rising sun and setting moon*
>
> *Pattern spoken, Witch's rune.*
>
> *Rising moon and setting sun*
>
> *Gold and silver move as one.*
>
> *As above and so below*
>
> *Just to think can make it so!"*

Using Your Magickal Powder

Once activated, the magickal powder has a compendium of uses, including sprinkling on poppets, conjuring bags, spell candles, altars, sachets, magick pillows, or corn dollies. Powders are scattered in the footsteps of an individual, across where they walk, or even under the sick bed. Many powders (if the ingredients are known) can be added to your favorite incense or thrown into the hearth fire or religious bonfire. Powders can also be offered to Spirit or deity in small bowls or placed at the quarter and cross-quarters of a circle to enhance elemental alignment, or be mixed directly into holy water and magickal inks (you can strain the mixture, but it isn't necessary).

Too, powders are known to be extremely useful when conjuring the dead or exorcising nasty spirits. An exorcism powder of this nature normally includes angelica, salt (negative things hate salt), eggshells, and lilac fragrance placed on a mirror. Some recipes for

one

two

three

four

five

✸

136

ghostbusting include mothballs, but these are highly toxic to children and pets and not recommended for the family magickal cabinet. Recipes for conjuring the dead almost always contain wormwood, which is considered toxic by the FDA and therefore should be handled with care.

Finally, magickal powder recipes can easily be turned into loose incense (though watch those toxic herbs). This can be accomplished by several methods:

- Place a small amount of powder directly on a charcoal tab (made for incense).

- Mixing a small amount of charcoal tab directly in the powder; burning on a tab is then not needed.

- Mixing a base wood treated with a saltpeter and water formula, left to dry, and then added to the powder (this is messy and painstaking). No charcoal required.

- Blending the powder with Makko and water and fashioning into a cone. Also messy.

A Bit o' Fire Magick—One Technique, Three Variations

The following exercise(s) incorporates one pillar candle in the color you desire (white is good for the first time if you are unsure of the color); paper; a magickal powder mixture of your making (prepared as previously discussed); the choice of a magickal sigil, symbol, or words that focuses on your desire; a stylus for carving a design on your candle; incense; a fire-safe cauldron; and a magickal oil for dressing the pillar. I have provided two additional designs for you to choose from, one for success in life that incorporates the star, and one for money magick with a basket theme. Both are variations of Pennsylvania Dutch quilting designs; however, you will be required to create a sigil of your own that will work in tandem with those I have provided.

one

two

three

four

five

137

Write your desire on a plain piece of paper. In a magick circle, bless all tools, including the stylus that you will use to carve the candle. Take the first letter of each word of your written desire and transfer that letter to scratch paper. Once you have all the letters, move them around in a pleasing design where all the letters somehow connect. As you create your sigil, keep in mind your desire. If you become frustrated in any way, acknowledge where that frustration is really coming from—is it the issue at hand? Is it something else? Mentally note your feelings and move on.

Using the stylus, transfer your sigil to the surface of the candle. Carving a candle is easy if you keep in mind that the procedure isn't going to be done in five minutes or less and that pressing hard will destroy the candle. Draw the initial design lightly on the candle, then go back over small areas, a bit at a time, until you reach the groove level you desire. This literally can take hours, depending on how exotic your design might be. Take your time. As you work, allow this to be a relaxing experience. Listen to pleasing music if you like. Add a chant to positively reinforce your work when your mind begins to wander or your brain attempts to spin out negative scenarios or unhappy emotions surface as you are working out your problem. The candle is a solution-oriented vehicle and your actions, thoughts, and emotions should support that. This exercise is also excellent to train students in the longevity of a focused working. As you work, use a soft cloth to buff the edges of your design. This will remove excess wax bits and raise a nice sheen to the work; it is also a mental cleansing and refining process. Allow the energy to flow in a pleasing way. Do not be frustrated if the stylus slips—incorporate that into the design, just as you smooth the mistakes in life into the mastery of your overall self.

Next, choose one of the designs (or a different one) on page 140 to add to your own sigil.

one
two
three
four
five

138

Carefully link this design to your own, which may take several hours to complete. In this case, it takes as long as it takes, and if you need to take a break, that won't deter from the overall working. When your candle is finished, buff the surface one last time, then place the pillar in the center of your altar until the correct moon phase or other timing vehicle you wish to use moves into place. You may want to cover your candle with a white or black cloth in the meantime; also, don't let anyone handle the pillar and if you think this is a possibility, wrap the candle in the cloth and store it in a safe place. Theoretically, you have already begun the magick and worked several hours on your candle in preparation for the lighting ceremony, which takes little time to perform. Having someone else touch the candle brings a wild card into the working, and this is also a sign that, for good or ill, the person who handled the pillar will somehow be involved in the solution-oriented result.

When you are ready to light the candle, the standard magickal procedures apply, including creating sacred space or casting a circle, calling the quarters (if you desire), grounding and centering, etc.

Here we are going to incorporate the stylus you used to originally carve the candle as your magickal wand. Dot the stylus tip with a bit of magickal oil. Envision the stylus glowing with power. With the stylus tip pointing outward, cast a magick circle, walking clockwise around the altar or desk, saying, "I conjure thee, O circle of art, to be for me a place of love, trust, peace, and joy, where no negativity can enter herein. A place of perfection where my words will manifest and my desires will be met! So mote it be!" Tap the other end of the stylus on the desk or altar (not the point) four times to seal the circle. Slowly rub your magickal powder into the design that you carved while holding the candle over the cauldron (so you don't make a mess). When you are satisfied with the results, lightly dot the design with magickal oil (not too much) and say firmly, "Creature of wax and wick, pattern of sigil and shape! By air

one

two

three

four

five

139

one

two

three

four

five

❖

140

These sigils are variations of Pennsylvania Dutch quilting designs: the left one is for money magick with a basket theme; the right one, which incorporates the star, is for success in life.

and fire, water and earth, I conjure thee to come to birth! The shape is made, the words begun, by power of stars and moon and sun, my will take form, success is won, as I do say it shall be done!" Light the candle on the word "done." With the light of the candle, draw an invoking pentagram over the altar, specifically the cauldron. Place the candle in the cauldron. Imagine the design you carved and any words you wrote taking shape, coalescing and lifting off the candle in a pattern of beautiful pulsating light, moving up and to the right and out into the universe to capture your need. Don't forget to release the circle.

Allow the candle to burn completely. When the candle is finished, place some of the powder and some of the wax in a small bag. Dot this bag with magickal oil and tie it shut. Add an empowered lodestone or crystal to boost the power. Carry it with you until you receive your desire. If the request is of a large nature, you can burn a single white or yellow votive candle each night for seven nights, or every Sunday. Place the bag by the candle while it burns. Envision a golden net springing from the bag and capturing your desire. When your desire is met, cleanse the lodestone and crystal, then burn the bag and contents, thanking the gods.

How to Make Magickal Potpourri and Fine Herbal Blends

Like powders, magickal potpourri and herbal blends are considered best if they are high in fragrance, bright in color, and the ingredients are chosen for the magickal intent. Unlike magickal powders, potpourri and herbal blends should be aged in dark glass jars (amber or cobalt work well) to ensure the overall scent permeates throughout the mixture. The equipment is much the same: Large glass or wooden bowls (powders don't need such big containers), wooden spoons, glass measuring cup, fragrance or essential oils (with a separate dropper for each oil), the herbs, and the dark jars for aging

one
two
three
four
five

141

and storage. Most magickal blend mixes have seven, nine, or eleven different ingredients (not including the oils); however, I have made (depending upon the situation) extremely complicated blends, including a twenty-one-herb recipe that also includes several oils. This super blend is used for ceremonial services.

Like powders, making magickal blends and potpourri lend themselves well to the lesson environment—teaching the student the properties of the herbs, magickal correspondences, and introducing them to the raw texture and aroma of the ingredients. Because blends and potpourri should be aged, they can be made well ahead of a particular ceremony, sabbat, etc., and incorporated into a group project night. Herbs are cheaper purchased by the pound; however, if ordering your supplies on the 'net, keep in mind that "c/s" means cut and sifted, "w" means whole, and "p" means powdered. You don't want powdered herbs for this type of project. You might also go for the higher-end pricing, choosing either organics or the better quality herb as cut and color are much better. A magickal blend can truly be enchanted eye candy in a ritual setting, especially if it is placed in a clear glass bowl or jar with a variety of gemstones accented by candlelight, or scattered around a favorite ritual statue. Wax talismans in a variety of colors and shapes can also give your potpourri an interesting magickal twist, especially if made by yourself or a magickal person for the purpose intended.

one

two

three

four

five

142

How to Blend the Blends

Measure and mix the heavier roots, barks, and spices first, adding the lighter ingredients, such as florals and leaves, second. Weigh this mixture and calculate 20 percent of that weight. This is the amount of your chosen fixative (orris root and oak moss are excellent—orris root is heavier) you will use to hold the scent of the herbs and the essentials or fragrance you choose to add. Mix the fixative thoroughly with your blend. Finally, add your essential blend (better to make the blend first rather than experimenting on the mixture) a few drops at a time until you attain the aromatic scent you desire. Pour the finished potpourri into the glass jars, cap tightly, and shake. The blend should age four to six weeks. Remember to shake the blend at least once a week to dispense the aroma throughout the herbs.

There is only one exception to this process and that is if you plan to activate the blend before you age it. As with powders, the activation can include bourbon, white rum, magickal sprays, or scented waters—even highly aromatic black coffee is sometimes used. This activation requires an extra step: spread the herbal blend on a screen. Spray lightly and allow it to dry thoroughly before you place it in the jar. If the blend is still wet when stored, the herbs will most likely rot.

Herbal blend formulas are also a great way to empower and store various gems, stones, shells, and metal talismans. If you don't want to put the stones through the mix, place them in the bottom of the jar first.

Herbal Blend Recipes

DREAMER'S DELIGHT for enhancing psychism, meditation, peaceful dreams, and for reducing nightmares.

> 5 ounces lavender flowers (element of air)
>
> 4 ounces prime rosebuds
>
> 2 ounces blue malva flowers (water)
>
> 1 ounce rosemary (fire)
>
> 3 ounces whole cloves (fire)
>
> 3 ounces catnip (water)
>
> 1 ounce yucca root (water)
>
> 1 ounce orris root (water)
>
> Essential oils/fragrance: lavender and violet (choose the balance you prefer—easy on the lavender to enhance the violet, or use lavender and sage

one
two
three
four
five

143

Blue diamond glitter can be used as an enhancement

½ pound crystal points (these you will use again after you have dispensed with the blend)

CEREMONIAL BLEND is a cleansing/success mixture used to entice good spirits.

one

two

three

four

five

144

4 ounces dried orange peels (better if you dry these yourself, they will retain more of their aroma)

4 ounces dried lemon peels (again, better if you dry these yourself)

4 ounces calendula (marigold); again, from your own garden they will be brighter than purchased by a supplier

3 ounces German chamomile (high grade)

2 ounces lemon verbena (whole leaves, if possible)

1 ounce orris root

1 ounce white beans

3 ounces frankincense, pounded to release aroma

20 drops lemon or lemon verbena oil

Amber chunks (these you will wish to reuse, as amber is extremely expensive)

Optional: Gold glitter

Optional: Spray with white rum and allow to dry before storing

GODDESS OF THE GLEN for personal empowerment, esbats, and prayers to deity. Nice to use for prayers and petitions involving children and animals.

3 ounces high-grade rosebuds

3 ounces angel wings

3 ounces patchouli

2 ounces hibiscus petals

1 ounce lavender

2 ounces cedar shavings

Essential oil: Patchouli or rose geranium

Optional: ½ pound moonstones

Cauldron-Simmering Potpourri

Originally designed to restore moisture in the air for wood-burning homes, these special blends mix the magick of earth, air, fire, and water in an extremely pleasing way and are perfect for solitary or group cauldron magick. They are excellent, too, to fill your kitchen or dining room with fragrant aroma on a late winter afternoon or brisk fall evening. Not all herbals lend themselves well to simmering potpourri (some are downright stinky), so be sure you test your latest wonderment before you whip up a batch of strange-smelling stuff that permeates the house for days (I did this—ahem. The comment from my children was, "Well! You can certainly tell a Witch lives here!") Simmering potpourri/blend mixes releases their aroma through steaming water. If you put them on the stove without the water they'll burn, and if you let the mess go dry over the heat you'll ruin your pot (okay, so I've done this, too). You can boil these blends directly on the stove in an old pot filled with water, in a cauldron over an outdoor fire, in a fire-safe bowl over a candle (such as a tea candle), or in electric potpourri burners made for this purpose. You can throw the mixture right in the pot loose with the water or immerse a white cotton bag stuffed with the mix and tied securely in the water. In a pinch I've even used a coffee filter twisted at the top (hey, it worked). For an extra sweet zest at the time of use you can add fresh fruit, such as apple slices and sliced citrus, to the bubbling brew!

one

two

three

four

five

145

Herbals that lend themselves well to simmering blends are:

Allspice	Ginger root
Anise	Galangal (only a little)
Apple slices (dried)	Juniper berries
Bay leaf	Lavender
Caraway seed	Lemon verbena
Cardamom	Nutmeg
Cedar chips	Mint
Cinnamon sticks	Rosemary
Citrus fruits	Sage
Cloves	Sandalwood (red or white)
Coriander seed	Tonka beans
Deerstongue	Vanilla beans
Eucalyptus	Wintergreen
Fennel seed	Woodruff

Fixatives for simmering potpourri blends include orris (some people like to powder it—I don't, but it is hard to find it cut and sifted from suppliers) and dried apple pieces and dried citrus peels, although they are added to the mixture differently than with the normal herbal potpourri blend. Again, the apple and citrus works better if you have dried them yourself, both aromatically and magickally. Set your fixatives aside and add your essential oils only to the fixative mixture, not the simmering blend (fragrance isn't a great idea because not all fragrances burn as well as they naturally smell—again, the voice of experience). Age the fixative for three days in a glass jar before adding your simmering potpourri mixture. Shake well. This type of herbal blend is ready for simmering about four days after the potpourri is added to the fixative. It will, however, last longer. Keep tightly sealed until use.

one

two

three

four

five

146

Festival Formulas

SAMHAIN

1 cup star anise

1 cup allspice (whole)

1 cup orange peel (use to hold fragrance)

¼ cup orris root (use to hold fragrance)

1 cup woodruff

1 cup juniper berries

1 cup whole mace

1 cup whole cloves

7 cinnamon sticks

3 cups rosehips (scented or unscented,
     they are sold both ways)

3 handfuls bay leaves

Throw a sliced "live" apple in the pot when simmering for an increased autumn note, or use an apple fragrance on the fixative mix of your choice or a very small amount of patchouli essential oil (or both if you are brave). Excellent to simmer in the west quarter at your Samhain party or masked ball.

ABUNDANT YULE

I have used this recipe every year for the past seventeen years to keep my house smelling "holiday-tyme," keep the money flowing in, and keep the happiness as high as it can be.

1½ cups orange peel—use this as your fixative with pine
     (only a little bit) essential oil

½ cup cardamom pods

13 cinnamon sticks (one for each lunar month)

one

two

three

four

five

147

1 cup dried apple slices

½ cup mace

¼ cup allspice

¼ cup cloves

½ cup sandalwood

⅛ cup wintergreen

11 tonka beans (for mastery over your finances)

one

two

three

four

five

148

When ready to boil, add sliced fresh oranges with cloves stuck in the rinds. For more pizzazz, add just a hint of ginger root.

Essential oils of choice would be lemon, sweet orange, or tangerine (or a combination of all three). My family prefers tangerine since when they were small and money was tight, I always made sure to put tangerines in their stockings because when I was small and money was tight, my parents always put tangerines in my Yule stockings. It's a family tradition—what can I say? Eat enough spaghetti dinners when you are young and struggling and you'll totally understand the significance.

BELTANE FLORALS

That lusty month of May! It's here, it's here . . . that shocking time of year when Witches and Pagans always find a creative soul in the bunch to build the Maypole. Always. Never fails. I've been running Pagan events for over twenty years, and always find someone eager to construct the Maypole. It's just not a task people run away from. Go figure.

1 cup lavender (for peace and cleansing)

2 cups fragrant rosebuds (purchase the highest
quality possible; for love and secrets)

1 cup orange peel (use as the fixative)

1 cup oak moss (for stability)

1 vanilla bean (to bring future riches)

¼ cup allspice

5 cinnamon sticks (for movement)

¼ cup mint (for money)

Lilac or magnolia fragrance (check your brand on a test batch, as fragrances tend to smell differently when subjected to heat); rose could also be used.

SIMMERING SUMMER SOLSTICE

This one is really nice if you have an outdoor cookout, or place it in the center of the circle in a simmering cauldron.

1 cup cinnamon sticks

1 cup orange peel (again, best if you dry these yourself)

1 cup grapefruit peel

½ cup allspice

3 cups of prime lemon verbena (careful when you order this one)

1½ cups orange peel

⅓ cup cloves

½ cup ginger root

1 vanilla bean

How to Make Incense Prayer Papers

Victorian prayer papers, as their name implies, are shaped strips of paper used to make petitions and wishes to deity. As they smolder, the essential oil aroma drifts about the sacred area. To make your own prayer papers, you will need:

3 tablespoons saltpeter

3 cups boiling spring water

one

two

three

four

five

149

Essential oils—20–24 drops total

Paper shapes or strips—blotter or high rag content

Glass bowl

Steel spoon

Clothespins

Wire rack or screen

Newspaper

one

two

three

four

five

Dissolve saltpeter in boiling water. Cool in heat-resistant glass bowl (do not use plastic, wood, or metal). Say a cleansing prayer over the mixture. Add the essential oil blend of your choice. Empower the mixture for your specific desire by stirring slowly with a steel spoon in a clockwise direction, and then in a figure-eight motion. Cut blotter paper or card stock into pleasing shapes about the size of your palm. If you plan to use colored paper, check first to make sure the dye holds. Dip paper shapes in the scented water and hang to dry with clothespins on a wire rack or flat on an old window screen and set on newspaper. The excess liquid will drip onto the newspaper. Allow to dry. If your paper curls, simply place on a flat surface after the drying process is complete and press with a few heavy books. The best storage is a glass jar, but plastic bags will work for short periods of time. Dispose of any excess liquid carefully. Remove the newspaper immediately from your home and remember that saltpeter is a burning agent. Do not set it near an open flame, including burning candles or cigarettes. Papers will light, then smolder—they do not continue to flame like flash paper. If your papers were stored in plastic, you may wish to set them out in the open air a few hours before use to ensure dryness.

To use the papers, you will need:

A fire-safe burn bowl

Pen and ink

Prayer paper(s)

White candle or colored intention candle

Holy water

Lighter or matches

Magickal oil for dressing the candle

one

two

three

four

five

151

Write your desire directly on the prayer paper along with any sigils that you feel match your intention. With the prayer paper, draw a figure-eight or other magickal symbol in the air, concentrating on your desire. Dress the candle with chosen magickal oil and once again draw the figure eight in the air with the candle. Wrap the paper around the unlit candle and repeat the figure-eight motion. Say "Three times is the charm" and snap your fingers over the candle/paper. Unwrap the paper and place it on the altar. Put the candle in a fire-safe holder. Light the candle. Sprinkle the holy water in a large circle that encompasses the prayer paper, the candle, and the fire-safe dish. Seal by knocking on the altar top three times. Hold the prayer paper to your heart chakra, slowly move the paper out from your body, then say, "From me to thee, from heart to fire, from paper to fulfilled desire . . . I make it so!" Light one edge of the prayer paper and drop it into the burn bowl. Blow softly once onto the paper to instill the holy breath. The paper will flame and then continue to smolder until all the paper turns to ash. Allow the candle to burn completely. The ceremony is done! Scatter the ashes of the cooled petition outside to the winds. Note: This ceremony can be used in conjunction with any other magick, spellwork, rite, or ritual.

Walking with Spirits

The belief in saints, spirits, deities, archetypes, gods, goddesses, and assorted higher beings is often integral to the life of the magickal practitioner. They are rainbow bridges from the third dimension into the mysteries of all the others (however many there may be). In the following exercise I purposefully chose a spirit outside of the Wiccan religion so that the practitioner learns to walk in many worlds, not just one. Sometimes this is very hard for students to do, and they mentally and physically recoil at the idea of using a belief system (or a portion of one) to which they know little. This type of knee-jerk reaction is to assume that something "bad" will happen to them should they look outside the confines of their own belief system. Granted, the rule still applies of not calling up what you can't put down; however, there is enough information here on this particular "spirit" to meet the needs of the practitioner, and I chose an energy that specifically works well with priests and priestesses in general, regardless of your culture. Absolutely complicated, steeped truly in mystery, and utterly harmonic in form, the Voodoo vèvès are an exciting magickal vehicle to master.

Ayzian Working for Success

Ayzian is a Voudon lwa (spirit). She is not a goddess but is an energy in her own right—a cohesion of past primitive belief, symbology, and the collective unconscious of the business world and the priesthood.

Ayzian is the protector and teacher of all initiates and is one of the first lwa to be called in many Voudon ceremonies. Her main "color" is white, with silver as a secondary. Every line in the design has meaning, every form an exciting correlation to quantum physics. Study the design completely, taking your own notes on how you believe it works. When you are ready, draw the design yourself on

one
two
three
four
five

152

paper, or paint it on wood or clay. The time it takes to re-create the design is a way for you to imbue yourself with the preparation of receiving your intended desire.

Offerings to this spirit include coconut, palm fronds (her symbol), white beans, calamus herb, white grapes, spring water, white grapes, beer, perfume, and silver and pure white objects. Her altar cloth should always be white. Candles can be white or silver. Clear spring water should accompany any offering. Keep in mind that once you give something to a lwa, it cannot be taken back. It belongs to that spirit forever. Fresh food should remain on the altar for only twenty-four hours. Offerings can be placed outside with petitions inserted in them and left to deteriorate in their own time. Vèvès are one way of contacting a specific lwa. Each lwa has his or her own specific pattern that must be activated to work. These patterns are based on the harmonics of sound and energy. In this spell the vèvè is activated twice: first to begin the vibratory pattern, and then, once the candle and the offerings are placed, to meld the energies of the vèvè to the offerings that represent your desire.

To begin, sprinkle the four directions of the paper from left to right and top to bottom with holy water. Activate the vèvè using a rattle to trace the pattern. The sound of the rattle following the lines brings the pattern to life. Next place your offerings at any of the star points. The top star point is reserved for your white or silver candle. Place your written petition under the fire-safe candleholder. Don't forget to dab the candle with magickal oil and sprinkle a bit of magickal powder on the candle and a bit on the design.

Before melding the energies, give thanks to your ancestors and say your favorite prayer or invocation. Ask that Spirit meld with your higher self and that your actions result in the greatest good. Light the candle. Trace the pattern of the vèvè again, beginning where Spirit leads your hand and continuing until you feel energized and full of power. Then blow three times on the vèvè (do not

one

two

three

four

five

153

one

two

three

four

five

154

Ayzian design for success.

blow out the candle) to instill holy breath. Seal with three shakes of the rattle. Thank the lwa and what you consider to be the Great Spirit. You are finished. Allow the candle to burn completely.

The spirit of Ayzian wants you to succeed in the marketplace. She absolutely loves the busy, upbeat energy of buying and selling. If you treat her well, she will respond accordingly. I have experienced her power from exceptionally high bids on eBay, to large sales when I really needed them on my website, to finding money to pay unexpected medical bills. Much luck in your partnership with this amazing lwa!

one

two

three

four

five

155

Summary

The exercises in this section included analyzing the data given on magickal powders and herbal blends and considering their import for using the physical gifts of this dimension to create positive, spiritual changes in the life of the practitioner. Here we discussed the dynamics of the tools and how they can be used. Only a few recipes were given—just enough to support the application but not an overabundance, so the focus is kept. From learning to create prayer papers for deity and then stepping outside the normal confines of Wicca, we learn to acknowledge and implement various occult teachings without fear of reprisal, as long as we do the appropriate research. In the next part we will dig further into the rich soil of the universe.

FIVE

Exercises in This Section

A Witch's Herbal

" O most powerful spirit of the bush with fragrant leaves, I am here again to seek wisdom. Give me tranquility and guidance to understand the mysteries of the forest and the knowledge of my ancestors."[1]

The Divine Rose

There is an old spell that goes something like this: If you are in need of anything, place a dried rose of Jericho in a clear bowl of clear water at 3 o'clock on a Friday afternoon. Leave the rose in the water for three days, praying each day at precisely 3 o'clock over the rose for what you desire. On the fourth day (the number four to seal the spell), remove the flower at 3 o'clock in the afternoon. Sprinkle the water from the bowl in every corner of your house; as you do so, envision white light and sparkling, positive energy entering the home on luxurious waves, bringing peace, prosperity, and harmony into your life.

Simple folk spells such as this are laden with history, correspondences, and associations that are not readily apparent. This particular formula is designed to draw amorphous or material objects toward the seeker, and we can see this correlation in a number of areas throughout the formula. Let's start with the flower. In earlier portions

---

1. Manuel Cordova-Rios, shaman trained in the Peruvian Amazon Basin. From Muller-Ebeling, Claudia, Christian Ratsch, and Wolf-Dieter Storl. *Witchcraft Medicine: Healing Arts, Shamanic Practices and Forbidden Plants*. Rochester, Vermont: Inner Traditions, 2003, page 171.

of this book we discussed the many levels the rose has in magickal applications—unfoldment, secrecy, the sacred spiral, the fact that energy moves in waves, and that there is a golden proportion in much of nature. The rose is a symbol of the magickal gateway between the manifest and the unmanifest. It is a prime three-dimensional example of bringing energy into physical form. The rose of Jericho also has religious connotations of its own and is unique in that, once dried properly, it can be revitalized by placing the plant in clear water. Like magick, this rose appears to be risen from the dead, a remarkable natural occurrence.

Yet there is much more in the spell. The bowl speaks of the magick circle in the natural field in which the practitioner will work. The clear water is associated with purity. And then there is the number three, representing our three-dimensional world, the ability of taking two opposing forces and combining them into a third force, the indication that some type of merger is necessary to create any given manifestation and, of course, the more loose association to a triple deity force. Naming the day—Friday—brings in astrological correspondences including the planetary energy of Venus in the elemental energies of earth and air, as Venus rules both Virgo and Libra. Friday is also associated with beauty, abundance, the arts, and fast cash. This day is often used for love spells and general monetary workings. If we look at this spell head-on, it is as much a cleansing working as it is a manifestation formula.

Finally, the number four speaks of security, stability, the four elements and, by the act of removing the flower, it incorporates the sealing process of the spell. We also know, scientifically speaking, that water can be digitized by thought. Praying over the water, then, actively charges the liquid with positive vibrations that are in turn scattered throughout the environment by the practitioner as he or she sprinkles the water in the home. The entirety of the spell contains only 103 words. The explanation, which is a shortened version,

one

two

three

four

five

160

is over 400 words. Like an iceberg, there is a lot beneath even the simplest of spells.

Looking at the older spells, those written a few hundred years ago, even sixty years ago—what might you see that you didn't recognize before?

Spell Review

Knowing this, as the first exercise in this section, I suggest that you pull out a few of your old spell books and take a look at them again. Choose three or four spells. Write them down and pull them apart with this same type of analysis. You may be incredibly surprised at what you find. Do additional research on symbols, history, etc., if this piques your interest. If you have been writing your own spells, you may wish to go back over your work with a deeper understanding of the process. I bet that you will discover your subconscious mind added great depth to your simplest working, or perhaps you will choose to add additional features. Finally, choose three spells that did not work in the way that you had planned and, considering your style and magickal practice, brainstorm about how you could change those spells to cultivate the original desire.

A Witch's Herbal

The following section, which takes up most of this part, contains over one hundred herbs and simple spell ideas that go with them. The first four parts of this book have given you step-by- step preparations for this material. In our journey we have learned to cleanse, empower, plan, and actively move beyond the limited box of everyday function in a sequential format designed for the self-taught or the individual who wishes to teach others. We have covered the basics in an interesting way, perhaps shifting into a different gear to get there. When I first began writing this section I spent three thousand dollars at various herbal suppliers and it took three years to

one

two

three

four

five

161

compile my data. I wanted to know what every herb looked like, smelled like, and how it behaved with other herbs in magickal applications. I was determined that I would learn how to blend the herbal kingdom in various combinations. As there are over 3,800 species worldwide, I guess I have a way to go, but at least there is plenty here to get you started. Enjoy!

one

two

three

four

five

✤

162

AGRIMONY *(Agrimonia eupatoria).* Along with elder flower, agrimony is most often used to break hexes and send them back to their original creator, therefore this is definitely a "karmic" herb. Sometimes called the "goblin breaker," the plant is used in many exorcism/cleansing and banishment rituals, especially when you obtain a new (to you) home or apartment. Also used to banish rotten apartment neighbors. Place herb in a muslin bag with other banishing plants and rub it against the wall or floor that you share with the undesirable individual(s) or scatter it on their doorstep with nettles, especially if you believe they are psychotic or "not of this world" (really). Add it to spells or rituals where peaceful sleep is necessary, or just peace in general. Dip a mini-broom in glue and coat with an agrimony, lavender, and rosemary mixture sprinkled with purple glitter to banish nightmares. Add a decorative bow and hang it over the headboard of your bed. *Planetary Energy: Jupiter. Elemental Energies: Fire, Water. Astrological Signs: Sagittarius, Pisces.*

ALFALFA *(Medicago sativa).* Many of us have had very lean times. Used in spellwork, alfalfa is said to assist in bringing prosperity into the home, especially in the form of food. Wrap it in a piece of white bread and draw the Feoh rune ($\digamma$) in the air over the bread, then place it on the altar with a white emergency candle (if you don't have food, you don't have money for candles—even a birthday candle will do.) An herb of plenty, add it to your emergency money jar to keep from "running dry" and to ward against poverty. Grind it with cinquefoil, almonds, and honeysuckle for a raise. Use it as an ingredient in a business success mixture that includes red clover. Sprinkle it around a candle dressed with a money-attracting magickal oil to attract positive success and energy in a creative endeavor. *Planetary Energy: Venus. Elemental Energy: Earth. Astrological Sign: Taurus.*

ALLSPICE *(Pimenta dioica).* Extremely popular in southern magickal applications, seen as a good luck charm, liked for its fast activation correspondences in money, love, and success. Mix it with frankincense, myrrh, and a stick of cinnamon in a pot of boiling water to fill the house with the aroma of warmth and happiness, banishing fears (especially on cold, wintry days). If you need a bit of luck in your life, fill a fire-safe bowl with allspice and brown sugar sprinkled on top with marigold or chamomile (or both). Ring with large quartz crystal points in a sunburst pattern. Activate it with a bell rung eleven times. *Planetary Energy: Mars. Elemental Energy: Fire. Astrological Sign: Aries.*

AMERICAN MANDRAKE *(Podophyllum peltatum).* Hathor's herb, known in Germany as "the sorcerer's root." Mandrake is definitely an herb of physical manifestation, whether we are talking about money, a new car, replacing the refrigerator that likes to freeze the eggs even though they are on the lower shelf or the washing machine that screams in fear when the laundry basket draws near. From skateboards to clothing, any spell conjured for the need of a physical item should include at least a little mandrake. For more drawing power (like you are trying to manifest a car or a house), try adding blue vervain, damiana, and a lodestone to the spell. This herb is another one of those items that the FDA considers unhealthy for

one

two

three

four

five

163

human consumption, so be sure to keep it locked in your magickal cabinet and away from children and pets. From the May apple family, this magickal herb is also used to coalesce your work and bring it into the physical plane even though the situation you are working for is not a solid item. Mandrake is also used to solidify love magick, increase monetary gain, and protect an establishment from financial loss. American mandrake and European mandrake are not the same plant; however, magickally they are interchangeable. *Planetary Energy: Saturn. Elemental Energy: Earth. Astrological Signs: Capricorn, Aquarius (classical).* SEE ALSO Mandrake.

one

two

three

four

five

✣

164

ANGELICA *(Angelica archangelica).* Root. Angelica is a member of the parsley family and is often found in rich, wet soil. Sometimes called masterwort (but be careful, it may not be the same) or archangel, the root portion of the plant is most commonly used in medicinal and magickal applications, although if you have a chance to "wildcraft" (find it yourself), the entire plant can be dried and used for magickal purposes. Think "higher-vibratory" work and you are definitely applying the right association. In magick, its correspondences include inspiration, wisdom, knowledge, success, gain, astral work, contacting spirit guides, and asking for divine intervention. When it gets deep—grab the angelica for magickal work! In Pow-Wow the root is used in breaking hexes and exorcising all manner of nasties. Hoodoo also has a variety of uses for this herb, including waters blended to bless babies, conjuring bags employed to "control your man," and powders ground to bless a home. Because this plant contains a compound much like estrogen, traditional folk magick generally includes this herb for any enchantments involving "women's difficulties." I've seen spells with bloodroot and angelica combined to assist women with menstrual problems. For menopausal difficulties, mix angelica with black cohosh and place in a blue conjuring bag with any blue gemstone. Hold the bag during daily meditations. Tie it together with nine knots to devil's shoestring and hang it above a doorway with a conjuring bag full of rue to keep undesirable people and energies from entering your home. Angelica root is tough and hard, not soft and pliable like some herbs; however, it is one of the first plants I learned to use in an exorcism ritual many years ago and I always make sure I have a bit on hand—you never know when you are going to need it! *Planetary Energy: Sun. Elemental Energy: Fire. Astrological Sign: Leo.*

one

two

three

four

five

ARNICA FLOWER *(Arnica montana)*. Popular in herbal mixes for their visual effect, arnica flowers are excellent poppet and magickal sachet "stuffing" herbs. Excellent for love and movement magick. *Planetary Energy: Mars. Elemental Energy: Fire. Astrological Sign: Aries.*

BAYBERRY BARK *(Myrica cerifera)*. Bayberry, barberry, and bay are not the same—they are three different plants, each with their own herbal and magickal properties. The bayberry is a hardy perennial evergreen shrub, popular among northern coastal states. When considering the magickal properties of a plant I always look to the growing process of the plant itself. The bayberry plant survives in lousy soil and withstands tremendous ocean storms, which tells us that, like the willow, the bayberry bush is a tenacious creature. From a candlemaking point of view, it takes one bushel of bayberries to make four pounds of wax, which equates to four medium-sized pillar candles or about twenty-eight votives. The bayberries are boiled and the wax skimmed from the top of the water in a long, tedious process. If a bayberry candle is expensive, it probably comes from this process. If it is relatively cheap, the scent is most likely synthetic. Bayberry candles using wax from the bayberry plant are extremely coveted in magick circles as bayberry's primary enchantment correspondences relate to money, financial wizardry, and prosperity throughout the year. Although the bark of the bayberry can be ground for incense, it does not produce a strong odor like the wax from the berries but it does carry the necessary magickal properties for any working associated with the plant; it is an excellent addition to any financial type of working. The bark of the bayberry is used in all manner of magick involving monetary windfall, prosperity, good fortune, family harmony and stability, good luck, and sympathy in partnership. Seasonally it is used with mistletoe, oak, and holly for Yule celebrations. Mix bayberry bark, nutmeg, cinnamon, cinquefoil, a magnet, and mistletoe for a fragrant money poppet or sachet. Roll this combination in a twenty-dollar bill and anoint with a money-magnet magickal oil. Wrap with a red thread and carry it in your pocket during holiday shopping to draw the "good deals" toward you. *Planetary Energy: Mercury. Elemental Energies: Earth, Air. Astrological Signs: Virgo, Libra.*

BEE POLLEN. Not exactly an herb or a resin, bee pollen is a must-have if you are involved in group magickal work, if you are on a team of any kind, or if business is slow and you need a nice push of added income from that buzzing hive of customers. Whether you are trying to stop an argument between several members in a group environment or if you are attempting to get a group to work better and faster, this particular magickal device can be extremely useful. Mix with real honey and gently spread on the bottom of a candle for increased wealth (remember, however, that the candle should be placed in a fire-safe container so you don't have a bonfire by the end of the working). Bee pollen can be mixed with any

one

two

three

four

five

166

herb grouping as a blender of energies, much like myrrh resin. For example, if you feel that the Saturn energy and Moon energy don't mesh the way you would like, add the bee pollen for a smoother blend. Use in spells to increase your divination skills and overall telepathic ability. Finally, bee pollen works extremely well in protective, compelling, or banishing spells. Use to get someone off their duff and the work in your hands. *Planetary Energy: Sun. Elemental Energy: Fire. Astrological Sign: Leo.*

BENZOIN *(Styrax benzoin).* Derived from vegetation native to Sumatra and white or eggshell in color, benzoin is milder than other resins and carries a vanilla scent (not overpowering). Often added to a variety of herbal mixes designed for loose burning. Used primarily in magick for harmony, protection, and psychic pursuits, it may be combined with copal for continued happiness. Use in handfasting sachets and gris-gris bags for advancing one's mental acuity (add peppermint to the sachet for increased clarity). Make into a loose incense with frankincense resin to burn on charcoal tabs for continued prosperity, or boil in a small pot of water for a pleasant, cleansing aroma during ritual. *Planetary Energy: Venus. Elemental Energies: Earth, Air. Astrological Signs: Taurus, Libra.*

BERGAMOT *(Monarda fistulosa).* If you need to generate more income, then bergamot is the herb for your magickal applications. Put your bank statement, paycheck stub, and other financial papers that indicate your intake of cold, hard cash in a cookie jar and sprinkle with bergamot, red clover, and mint. Add gold glitter and a magnet or lodestone. Cap. Lace top of jar with a magickal money-drawing oil. Place a green candle on top and let it sit for one full week, then burn the candle for seven minutes, turn it upside down, and extinguish it on the

one
two
three
four
five

167

lid of the jar, saying, "Good fortune is here!" *Planetary Energy: Sun. Elemental Energy: Fire. Astrological Sign: Leo.*

BETHROOT *(Trillium erectum).* Primarily used in love spells to gather and coalesce the "forces of harmony." Combine with rose petals, lemon verbena, and lavender sprinkled with a touch of yohimbe powder and a piece of rose quartz or carnelian for a unique love-drawing charm. *Planetary Energy: Venus. Elemental Energies: Air, Water. Astrological Signs: Libra, Cancer.*

one

two

three

four

five

168

BIRCH LEAF *(Betula lenta).* As I was growing up, I discovered three particularly chatty trees in my area and at some point along the magickal way I learned that if you listen they will speak to you. The maple whispers tidings of joy and good fortune, especially in the depths of a soft summer night; the willow speaks of delicate mystery, and her favorite time centers on dusk; and the birch is a bit different—stately, seriously communicative, definitely a tree of well-formulated messages. His preferred hour appears to be at the first touch of morning, perhaps because his bark is distinctively white and glows in the dawn's golden rays. Indeed, the birch's song is so sweet as the sun peeks over the horizon that it might be mistaken for the first melody of a waking bird. With birch's association with light, it is not so surprising that some of the first candles were crafted of birch. Birch doesn't just purify—the energy of this tree brings us so much more! Dispelling the darkness! Scaring the shadows back to where they belong! Sweeping the area clean of negative debris! Add to a mixture of lavender, rosemary, and chamomile in a sleep sachet, especially if you are suffering from insomnia caused by worry or unhappiness caused by others. Should I go on? Destroying falsities, that's a good one. Mix with plantain and lobelia for a nasty case of gossip. Ritual cleansing—red sandalwood chips, hyssop, and birch is a very nice combination. If you are into conjuring weather magick and storms, legend has it that if you carry birch you won't be struck by lightening; however, I wouldn't test that theory. Finally, add birch to any conjuring bag when doing work against criminal intent or for protection for those "in service" (police officers, fire people, paramedics, soldiers). *Planetary Energy: Venus. Elemental Energies: Air, Earth. Astrological Signs: Libra, Capricorn.*

one
two
three
four
five
✳
169

BLACK COHOSH *(Cimicifuga racemosa).* Surprisingly enough, this herb is a member of the buttercup family! Sometimes called black snakeroot, but be careful here as the word "snakeroot" seems to cover a variety of plant species. Magickally considered highly protective and extremely lucky, black cohosh (another tough root like angelica) can be used in a variety of enchanting applications that range from protecting the home to female medical difficulties. Scatter around a red candle for spellwork involving conjuring inner courage. Mix with angelica, sprinkle on the floor, and sweep out the door to banish unwanted energies in the home. Add to any relationship spell to strengthen the love. If you've been having a run of bad luck, a Pow-Wow spell includes mixing black cohosh, rose petals, bay leaves, and lemon rinds in a cleansed dish. Then form herbs into the shape of a banishing pentacle on a white plate. Place near the front door. Remove when luck turns around. *Planetary Energy: Saturn. Elemental Energy: Earth. Astrological Sign: Capricorn.*

BLADDERWRACK *(Fucus versiculosus).* Sea kelp (which is what this is) is a magnificent money plant. I rate it right up there with cinquefoil. Wrap in red felt and soak in the most expensive bourbon you can afford to bring money. Let it dry thoroughly and carry it in your pocket or purse, or put it in a money-drawing jar along with a lodestone. Bladderwrack has other uses as well, including wind and weather magick. To command the winds, hold the herb in your hand, intone the words of power, and then throw it in the direction the storm is coming. Combine with feverfew for safe and healthy travel, including a protective gris-gris bag for your car, and definitely if you are flying. If you live by the sea, this plant is fairly easy to obtain, but if you are landlocked, you're stuck buying from a supplier. Empower when the Moon is in Cancer for more power. *Planetary Energy: Moon. Elemental Energy: Water. Astrological Sign: Cancer.*

BLESSED THISTLE *(Cnicus benedictus).* In antiquity, this plant was called the "bath of Venus" or the "lips of Venus," as rainwater collects in the leaf bases. Excellent pillow or poppet-stuffing herb (make sure weave of material is tight, due to the consistency of this plant). If you think nasty magick is afoot, mix blessed thistle, lobelia, and wormwood, especially if you know a rumor started it all and you want to trace it back to the source. Take these herbs, place them in a "trick" of felt, sew, douse with perfume, and deliver to the grave of your most famous female ancestor—one known for her honesty and integrity. You'll find the culprit soon enough! Empower a candle ringed with burdock and blessed thistle to dump a dunderhead out of your life. Blessed thistle has a compendium of uses in magick—healing, compassion, beauty, and protection in times of violence, war, or strife, to name a few; it is also used to ward thieves from a home or business, especially if empowered during the waning moon in Lunar Mansion 17 (when the Moon is between 25 degrees, 42 minutes of Libra and 8 degrees, 36 minutes of Scorpio). Add to healing spells to renew vitality and bring back that glow of health. In the sickroom of

one

two

three

four

five

170

cold and flu patients, place a cut onion on top of a mixture of echinacea, blessed thistle, and lavender to remove germs and negativity. Renew daily. *Planetary Energy: Mars. Elemental Energies: Fire, Water. Astrological Signs: Aries, Scorpio (classical).*

BLOODROOT (KING) *(Sanguinaria canadensis).* Unicorn root aside, bloodroot is one of the most expensive herbs on the market today. In weight the root is much heavier than most. In magick this is an herb of ultimate success, whether we are talking about love, money, or protection. It was once thought that if you rubbed your palm with the root that whomever you touched would fall under your spell (normally used in marriage proposals). This is another one of those herbs that the FDA considers inappropriate for human consumption; however, it was used at one time in toothpaste to remove plaque (go figure). According to my father, this plant was prevalent in the area when he was a child and he often collected the delicate white flowers from the nearby woods to give to his mother. I find this interestingly appropriate as one medieval correspondence for this plant is to generate universal love and open the pathway to communication through harmony and understanding by burning away all that is negative. If you wish to be king or queen of your pond, stock your magickal cabinet with bloodroot and give it a whirl in your spells. *Planetary Energies: Sun, Mars. Elemental Energy: Fire. Astrological Signs: Leo, Aries.*

BLUE MALVA FLOWERS *(Malva officinalis).* As most magickal herbs are either green, brown, or yellow, working with these pretty flowers adds a bit of color to your application and is especially nice if you are making a protective potpourri that will be in a clear glass jar and on display in your home. Related to althea and rose of Sharon, blue malva can be added to mixtures specifically designed for conjuring spirits and honoring

one

two

three

four

five

171

the dead. They are the flower to make "unseen" things seen (hidden agendas, lies, covert operatons, etc.). Like althea, blue malva can be instrumental in magick that involves finding treasure. Although you may think of the old-fashioned way of discovering treasure, allow your mind to expand beyond the word itself—finding information, the truth, your car keys, something stolen from you, a person—there are a compendium of uses if you just allow yourself to be creative! Blue malva flowers are an excellent addition to protective magick, as tiny fibers at the base of the flower tend to be prickly, which means that this is not an herb for a sleep pillow. Use care when crushing or mixing with other herbs; it is definitely not suggested for an herbal bath. Mix with nettles and graveyard dirt for an exorcism with a bit of punch. Part of the mallow family, use it in rituals around candles when you wish to meditate, practice grounding and centering, or when you are not focused due to stress and need that "still point" from which to launch your endeavors. *Planetary Energy: Moon. Elemental Energy: Water. Astrological Sign: Cancer.*

BLUE VERVAIN *(Verbena hastata).* Magickally this is a "must-have" (at least in my mind) in the cupboard, as blue vervain is the essence of Mercury—and when speed is what you need in magickal work, a pinch of this herb really seems to help. However, speed isn't the only energy in this versatile plant; you name it, there's probably a spell that has this herb in it. Pow-Wow practitioners used vervain with juniper berries to call back a stolen item to the original owner. Whether we are talking health, wealth, protection, or love, vervain certainly can make itself useful in your repertoire. Use with elecampane to conjure material objects, with lavender to prevent nightmares, or patchouli for a powerful love spell. In Pennsylvania folk magick, if you need money, bury a mixture of vervain and

one
two
three
four
five

❖

172

cinquefoil in your garden. Truly the enchanter's plant! *Planetary Energy: Mercury. Elemental Energy: Air. Astrological Sign: Libra.*

BONESET *(Eupatorium perfoliatum).* Primarily used in exorcism mixes, spells, and rituals, boneset is thought to drive evil spirits and negativity from any person or environment. As an herb of Saturn, it works well on nasty, cranky, older people who would rather take their life's failures out on you than make an attempt to grow into better, wiser individuals. It's definitely a great herb for those biddies on the job who just can't keep their noses in their own affairs, or the next-door neighbor who likes to know every iota of your business, viewing you as their daily entertainment. Combine with plantain and slippery elm to curtail gossip. *Planetary Energy: Saturn. Elemental Energy: Earth. Astrological Sign: Capricorn.*

BUCKTHORN AGED BARK *(Rhamnus frangula).* Found in the Carolinas and Virginia and out through Nebraska, buckthorn is high on the list when it comes to magick involving legal matters. From court cases to red-tape snafus, buckthorn is the most logical choice for the base herb in conjuring bags or candle magick. Lawyers, legal assistants, and those entangled in the "system" may find this herb particularly helpful. Add to fennel and fenugreek if you are hankering for a visit from a gnome or faery, as this herb is used to conjure such devas (have milk, honey, and your request in hand). *Planetary Energy: Jupiter. Elemental Energy: Fire. Astrological Sign: Sagittarius.*

BURDOCK *(Arctium lappa).* Burdock (also known as bat weed) is primary a spell-breaking herb, whether that spell was cast by yourself and brought an experience you didn't desire, was a spell cast by someone else, or was simply some nasty charismatic energy from a loony bird who has managed to flutter

one

two

three

four

five

173

and honk into your life. A protective herb in magickal applications, you can add this one to conjuring bags, sachets, and poppets for protecting people, places, and objects. This is a great plant to use in magick if you are trying to teach your students to ground and center or if you are having a problem keeping your feet on the ground. If you want someone to get serious about a situation, add this herb to your magick. *Planetary Energy: Venus. Elemental Energy: Earth. Astrological Sign: Taurus.*

one

two

three

four

five

✦

174

BUTCHER'S BROOM *(Ruscus aculeatus)*. If you are into weather magick, then broom is for you. To raise the winds, calm them, or call for fine weather or even a change in your life, add to bladderwrack and blow at the four quarters of an outside circle. If you need to blow out a destructive force, throw in lobelia; however, as both broom and lobelia are considered by the FDA to be unhealthy for human consumption, this should not be done inside the home (and for pity's sake, don't inhale before you blow)! In Hoodoo magick, if you need to calm a destructive force, mix with holy water, make a hole in the ground, stuff the hole with the problem written on a small piece of paper, pour the herb and water mixture over the paper, then cover with dirt. Other magickal applications for this herb include purification and exorcism. *Planetary Energy: Mercury. Elemental Energy: Air. Astrological Sign: Gemini.*

CALAMUS *(Acorus calamus)*. A Hoodoo favorite in money spells and excellent for magick involving protection during travel. More importantly, it is one of the three herbs that can be used to "set" a spell (or a smell). The other two herbs that can master this feat are orris root and oak moss. Calamus is said to have "commanding" abilities in the magickal world. Combine with alfalfa to keep hunger and poverty away from your doorstep. Use with the power herbs to add strength to any spell (especially echinacea). This herb primarily focuses on matters of the home and the safety of the family unit. *Planetary Energy: Moon. Elemental Energy: Water. Astrological Sign: Cancer.*

CASCARA SAGRADA (*Rhamnus purshiana*). From the buckthorn family. If you've got legal problems, the morning that you must go to court or to a legal appointment, place a mixture of celandine and cascara sagrada in a coffee filter. Plop in the coffee maker. Run one cup of hot water through the filter and allow the infusion to fill a bowl (not your coffeepot). Let cool. Sprinkle at every entrance of your apartment or home, the four corners inside the house, and the four corners of your property. Got someone hounding you, trying to force you legally to do something you don't want to do? Each day for seven days burn a brown candle atop a bowl of brown sugar mixed with cascara sagrada. Throw it in the dumpster on the eighth day, saying, "Eight is mastery—and I have now mastered the situation. Be gone! I am free!" (Eight is mastery of the physical, eleven is mastery of the spiritual, and twenty-one is mastery of both physical and spiritual.) This herb is also used in spells for meditation, spirituality incenses, and general protection magick. *Planetary Energy: Sun. Elemental Energy: Fire. Astrological Sign: Leo.*

CATNIP *(Nepeta cataria).* Used in attraction and animal magick (especially involving cats, though some puppies seem enamored with it as well). Catnip is used to gain friends and lovers in spells and rituals. A good luck herb, mix with calamus, linden, rose petals, and vetiver—add a lodestone or tonka bean in a sachet or gris-gris that can be used for success and harmony in almost any endeavor. For love, place on a red cloth with a lock of your hair, add rose petals, patchouli, and bloodroot, and sprinkle with a Mars-oriented magickal powder. Tie shut with

one

two

three

four

five

175

red or gold ribbon. *Planetary Energy: Moon. Elemental Energy: Water. Astrological Sign: Cancer.*

CAT'S CLAW INNER BARK *(Uncaria tomentosa).* Una de Gato. She yawns, stretches, and cuts a swath in the air with those razor-sharp claws, and you're very happy that she missed your nose. If you could handle that visualization, then you've got the essence of this herb—it looks like what's left when your cat gets done with a favorite toy: shredded. I used this in magick on the last fool that tried to mess with one of my kids. He ain't around no more. A great stuffing herb for poppets (though a bit coarse; if you want something softer, try blessed thistle), cat's claw is definitely a protection-oriented plant—it doesn't cower, it gets right out there with the lightening speed of your favorite kitty and puts up an excellent defensive front (at least in my experience). Where catnip is "charming," cat's claw carries adequate punch for some of those touchier magicks—especially when calling Bast and Sekhmet, the Egyptian cat goddesses who don't trifle with the little things in life. You won't find much about cat's claw in the old American and European magickal books (if you find anything at all) because it is from South and Central America, deriving its folk name from the nasty thorns the plant so proudly presents to the unwary human hand, and it has only recently entered the American market from the medical platform. Peruvian priests used this plant to eradicate disturbances between the body and the spirit, believing that this particular herb can realign the three bodies (physical body, mind, and soul) when used properly in a healing or ritual format. Today, the herb has gained popularity in some circles by improving the vitality in cancer patients, especially in those who have chosen chemotherapy, and suppressing tumor growth; however, from my research it is clear that many over-the-counter offerings of cat's claw are not always to be trusted,

one

two

three

four

five

176

as there are twenty different varieties of this herb and not all of them would help in this type of situation. Where medical findings go, so then does that of the magickal use of any plant. As our scientists learn more through chemical analysis and testing, so we, the magickal people, can extend our knowledge on the energy function of any plant. Cat's claw is an excellent example of one item that could be placed in a conjuring bag when working to reduce a tumor in healing enchantments. *Planetary Energy: Sun. Elemental Energy: Fire. Astrological Sign: Leo.*

CELANDINE *(Chelidonium majus).* Celandine's magickal thrust is to help you wiggle out of really tight situations. Combine with flax seed if you are really desperate. The primary herb of escape, it is often used in legal magick or spellcasting that involves unfair rules, regulations, and the unjust behavior of those in power. At the same time it is considered a protective device so that one remains as unscathed as possible. The herb is also placed in mixtures wherein protection is needed to avoid the label of scapegoat for a particular issue or issues, which occurs often in Fortune 500 companies (I've seen it firsthand), political groups, production lines, and warehouse environments. Of course, if this is happening to you, you might take the heads-up that Spirit is trying to tell you that you shouldn't be in this line of work. Celandine is also used in magickal mixtures for family happiness, especially if one partner is kitchen-sinking, suffering from mild depression, or projecting his or her ills on the other individual. If your hubby or wife is bringing the angst of work home, mix a tiny amount of celandine and basil in the washing machine's wash water (not the final rinse water) to remove all negativity and protect the family. *Planetary Energy: Sun. Elemental Energy: Fire. Astrological Sign: Leo.*

one

two

three

four

five

177

CHAMOMILE, GERMAN *(Matricaria chamomilla).* Along with lavender, chamomile is one of my favorite herbs. Anti-stress, fast cash, success, and anti-nightmare—this plant has a variety of uses in magickal work. Chamomile tea is often drunk by prospective students before their initiation or elevation ceremonies, before group meditation or hypnotherapy sessions. Considered an excellent spell-buster, chamomile mixed with pickling salt sprinkled around the edges of one's property was thought to protect the borders from thieves, vagabonds, and nasty sorcerers who would curse your riches. Salt, however, will kill your plants, so be careful where you sprinkle the mixture outdoors. In medieval Germany chamomile mixed with dandelion was ground together along with the representation of a toad and placed in a holy area to overcome illness, or prevent the miscarriage of anything from justice to a human being. *Planetary Energy: Sun. Elemental Energy: Fire. Astrological Sign: Leo.*

COLTSFOOT *(Tussilago farfara).* Sometimes called British tobacco or bull's foot, this herb has several magickal applications. Combine with healing herbs during the cold and flu season, especially eucalyptus. Stressful day? Mix with lavender and chamomile. Wanna hot time in the town tonight? Combine with patchouli. Also popular in rituals and magick associated with totem animals and calling alchemical animals. Coltsfoot is another "booster" herb, rarely used alone in southern magick, and added for additional power and longevity of the spell. *Planetary Energy: Moon. Elemental Energy: Water. Astrological Sign: Cancer.*

COMFREY *(Symphytum officinale).* Protection, safety, and anti-theft—the herb of "comfort" and stability. Mix with juniper berries to protect property and when on fun travel or business

one
two
three
four
five

❖

178

trips. Add to any money spell, especially when the Moon is in Taurus, for protecting your finances. Add to gris-gris bags for the protection of a senior citizen who is healing or recovering from illness or surgery. *Planetary Energy: Saturn. Elemental Energy: Earth. Astrological Sign: Capricorn.*

COPAL RESIN *(Bursera fagaroides)*, COPAL *(Hymenaea courbaril)*. From Central America and sometimes called Mexican frankincense, used by the Mayan culture as "food for the gods." Copal, a tree resin, comes in a variety of colors. Employed by modern magickal practitioners in spells and rituals focused on harmony, happiness, purification, good luck, prosperity, increasing the power of spells, meditation and mental training, and to break spells (someone else's or your own, in case you make a boo-boo). *Planetary Energy: Jupiter. Elemental Energies: Fire, Water. Astrological Signs: Sagittarius, Pisces.*

DAMIANA LEAF *(Turnera diffusa)*. A prime magickal ingredient in love spells, especially if mixed with patchouli and bethroot (trillium) and laced with your favorite love oil (or musk fragrance). However, if it is spirits you want to see and increase your psychic abilities, then many magickal recipes include this particular herb along with wormwood, deerstongue, and uva ursi. Like patchouli and dragon's blood, damiana can also be used as an extra ingredient to strengthen a spell, especially if you feel that the odds are slim to none that success may be slow to manifest. Most interesting, however, is damiana's role in Hoodoo magick—it is a "calling" herb and is thought to appeal to one's basic drives: food, sex, and survival. It is often used to call an errant lover home, although this is only one use for the calling. I would definitely use this herb in magickal work involving the finding of a lost or stolen pet (or person), though I suggest adding protective herbs as well to balance the

one

two

three

four

five

179

spell toward the individual's (or pet's) utmost safety. As all things have primal energy, the herb can also be used in calling lost objects to their original owner—include juniper berries and vervain if you feel the item was stolen. *Planetary Energy: Mars. Elemental Energy: Fire. Astrological Signs: Aries, Scorpio (classical).*

one

two

three

four

five

✢

180

DEVIL'S CLAW ROOT *(Harpago phytum procumbens).* If you need an herb in a spell focused on calming the angry side of life (yours or someone else's), then you'll probably want to throw this herb into the pot. A tough root, it is native to southern Africa, especially found in the Kalahari Desert, Namibia, and on the island of Madagascar. This plant drew its name from the herb's unusual fruits that are covered with small hooks. It is the tubers of the plant that are commonly sold in magickal and herbal stores, hence the tough nature of the item. Magickal correspondences include reducing the suffering and pain of loss and distilling anger. Devil's claw is a root of balance and therefore can be added to gris-gris bags that concentrate on harmony (inner and outer). Mix with hawthorn and pansy for family unity. If someone is being extremely acidic toward you, your family, or your work, cut a small tomato in half and hollow out a small pocket in one half. Place the offending individual's name inside the hollow covered with devil's claw, angelica root, and black cohosh. Sprinkle with holy water. Add white blitz (see part one) if the difficulty is extremely troublesome. Put the tomato back together and secure with two hat pins crossed like an "x" through the tomato. Place in the sun. As the tomato collapses, so sayeth the legend, so will the individual's anger toward you. Excellent for use in meditation that focuses on removing anger or fear from your lifestyle. *Planetary Energy: Moon. Elemental Energy: Water. Astrological Sign: Cancer.*

DEVIL'S SHOESTRING *(Tephrosia virginiana).* A member of the honeysuckle family, devil's shoestring is the primary magickal ingredient in most job and employment spells. Soaked in good bourbon, it is added to Hoodoo "tricks" for luck in gambling and money-attraction workings. A bit of the bourbon is also poured in a shot glass and offered to the gods when the herb is removed from the jar. Devil's shoestring is also used in gossip spells to keep the poison tongues of colleagues (or their relations), neighbors, or family members from filling your life with poisonous goop. Weave several pieces of the herb together with colorful ribbons and hang on your desk at work to protect your interests and show the boss that you deserve a raise. However, since the boss will be more attentive, it is best not to goof off. If you have a nosey neighbor who insists on watching your door like your affairs are a real-life television episode, tape empowered pieces of devil's shoestring to the windows and doors that face the neighbor's property. Remember to replace every thirty days. *Planetary Energy: Jupiter. Elemental Energy: Fire. Astrological Signs: Sagittarius, Pisces (classical).*

DRAGON'S BLOOD RESIN *(Calamus draco).* Much coveted in the world of the Witches, dragon's blood is extremely useful in dozens of spells and rituals. Known for more power, the herb is added to a compendium of enchantments. Dragon's blood is sold in chunks or in powdered form, which is more expensive because dragon's blood is a pain to granulate and is messy to boot. A little bit will do ya when it comes to this herb, which can be added to magickal ink formulas and wax. Dragon's blood resin will stain clothing. It can be rubbed on natural wood and then covered with sealer to lock in energies. Note: Dragon's blood is sticky and difficult to clean off any surface. Not recommended for a coffee grinder—use a rubber mallet

one

two

three

four

five

181

instead. Once broken, it is easy to pulverize with mortar and pestle. Whether you want more virility, passion, or power, this herb ought to do it for you. *Planetary Energy: Mars. Elemental Energy: Fire. Astrological Sign: Aries.*

ECHINACEA *(Angustifolia).* Where vervain speeds the spell and dragon's blood and patchouli add more power, echinacea strengthens the web of the magick itself. Popular in today's herbal healing market, echinacea is not a cure-all, but it does strengthen what you have. Therefore, if you are feeling ill or a little down, you might want to throw in a bit of echinacea to set the magickal application. *Planetary Energy: Mars. Elemental Energy: Fire. Astrological Sign: Aries.*

ELDER *(Sambucus nigra).* This herb is one of my favorites and I've been using it (both flowers and leaves) for years in protective magickal work. Used to break all manner of enchantments, it is an excellent ingredient in exorcism spells, banishing negative people and things, breaking bad habits, and sending evil energies back to where they belong. Called the bat's flower, this is definitely a gothic-type herb also used in mixtures for consecration and commanding things to go away. Also employed in crossing rituals and ceremonies where the dead are honored. Combine with feverfew for spells to ward off attackers and place in gris-gris bags to hang over the threshold of any home or business to ward the premises. Another Hoodoo favorite in the herb department. *Planetary Energies: Moon, Venus. Elemental Energies: Water, Earth. Astrological Signs: Cancer, Taurus.*

ELECAMPANE ROOT *(Inula helenum).* The sorcerer's choice, elecampane definitely brings the truth to light in magickal applications. Related to ploughman's spikenard and bitter weed in the aster family. Mix with dice in a wooden cup and shake it

one
two
three
four
five

182

at every quarter four times, then seven times in the center of the circle—works great! Combine with blue malva flowers and a tiger-eye gemstone for particularly sticky cases. Add to a divination gris-gris bag with uva ursa, wormwood, broom, hibiscus, and a nice moonstone to increase your psychic abilities. Also used in spells for healing the mind, especially after a difficult experience. Mix with mistletoe for love spells. *Planetary Energy: Mercury. Elemental Energy: Air. Astrological Sign: Gemini.*

EUCALYPTUS LEAF *(Myrtaceae)*. With more than 500 species of eucalyptus, this plant covers three-fourths of the Australian continent and was medicinally a prime ingredient in the treatment of malaria. A germicide known for its defense against colds and flu, treating abscesses, etc., it cannot be used at its full strength. The eucalyptus leaf is a magickal favorite for inclusion in healing spells, especially when working against contagious diseases. A simple healing mixture that includes garlic, chopped onion, and eucalyptus on a plate ringing a green candle in the sickroom works magickally as well as on the earth plane. Garlic and onion are natural air purifiers (although it smells *way* stinky). Use eucalyptus leaf in poppets and conjuring bags for sickness involving both body and mind. *Planetary Energy: Moon. Elemental Energy: Water. Astrological Correspondence: Cancer.*

EVENING PRIMROSE *(Oenothera)*. An herb of night magick, balance, and protection from all who plot against you, the evening primrose derives its name from the natural opening of its flowers just at sunset. Like moonflowers, the evening primrose is a plant of the devas, heralding the magick produced by the slanted rays of the sinking sun and reminding the enchantress that the dance is about to begin! Some magickal people believe that this herb is a great addition to the opening

one

two

three

four

five

183

of your ritual, drawing more power to the working and assisting in balancing those energies present for a harmonious focus, especially if you are doing a public group ritual where it is highly likely that several participants will not be "in tune" due to inexperience or outright rudeness. For the latter, evening primrose seems to shove them out of the circle environment so that they go elsewhere—as if the herb determines who is properly prepared and who is not. I've seen this happen, especially when the HPS wore a wrist sachet filled with this and other protective herbs on her dominant hand when casting the circle. Some dude dressed all in black, thinking he was all cool, stuck up his nose and stalked off. It was later learned that he was only present to "screw up the energies," just to prove to his friends that he could do so. *Not.* Interestingly enough, this particular flower is sometimes called "password." To attract devas, use in combination with lavender. To gain respect from others, try a gris-gris bag with sunflower petals, gold glitter, a lodestone, devil's claw, and damiana (both are considered "calling" herbs). *Planetary Energy: Venus. Elemental Energy: Air. Astrological Signs: Libra, Taurus.*

EYEBRIGHT *(Euphrasia officinalis).* This is the Hoodoo favorite for divination, clear sight, learning to "look beyond," and discovering the truth of any matter (sort of like a tiger-eye gemstone). Soaked in clear spring water, strained and empowered under a Full Moon or a Moon in Scorpio or Pisces, the solution is sometimes used to clean magickal mirrors and other scrying tools. Let settle in a steaming cup of hot water while you do your homework (yes, big people often are required to do homework), breathing in the aroma for a clear mind. Add to any divinatory formula or spells to encourage the flow of information. Also used in recipes for conjuring the dead. *Planetary Energy: Mercury. Elemental Energy: Air. Astrological Signs: Virgo, Gemini.*

one

two

three

four

five

❖

184

FAVA BEAN. Herbal charm. Sometimes called "the mojo bean," fava beans are thought to enliven magick and please the gods and spirits. Often given as offerings in money spells or placed in gris-gris bags to draw good fortune to the practitioner. Empowered beans are sometimes placed at the foot of statues (gods and saints alike). *Planetary Energy: Venus. Elemental Energy: Earth. Astrological Sign: Taurus.*

FENNEL *(Foeniculum vulgare).* From the parsley family, fennel has a licorice scent. Magickally, fennel is great for diffusing any volatile situation, especially if one of the individuals is just a bag of hot air! To take care of a braggart, blow up a balloon and carefully insert the blowhard's name along with empowered fennel. Tie. In circle, pop the balloon with an empowered nice, long, sharp, shiny pin over a white plate. Throw away balloon pieces and bury fennel and the name off of your property. On the lighter side of life, fennel is used to conjure faery magick: place a mixture of evening primrose, lavender, and fennel around a bowl of milk. Do the magick, scatter the herbs, leave the milk. Dragon magick also incorporates fennel. Place by a candle at each of the four quarters in a ritual circle to call them in. Some magickal practitioners mix rue, lavender, and juniper berries in a gris-gris bag with anti-theft charms to avoid vehicle confiscation. In Hoodoo, if you have been unfairly treated by a legal institution or government agency, fennel is a primary ingredient in several spells tailored to this unfortunate circumstance. Such spells often include black mustard seed, cascara sagrada (or buckthorn bark—both are from the same family), and oregano. Add rosebuds to keep your business private. *Planetary Energy: Mercury. Elemental Energies: Air, Earth. Astrological Signs: Gemini, Virgo.*

one

two

three

four

five

185

FENUGREEK *(Trigonella foenum-graecum).* Sometimes called "the banker's herb" in magickal communities, fenugreek's primary function is to draw money to the household or business in the form of cash, loans, bonuses, etc. Compound with a lodestone or magnet in a jelly jar and legend has it that you have double the power to draw financial success to you. Throw in alfalfa once a week for seven weeks, then remove the mixture from your home and start over again. First used by Egyptians, then brought to Europe in the ninth century by Benedictine monks, this herb works well in various financial and prosperity spells. In Hoodoo lore, a dried eggshell was filled with fenugreek, dirt from a prosperous establishment, and one shredded bill of any monetary denomination on a new moon, then sprinkled with honey and brown sugar to draw success to any business enterprise. After seven days the shell and contents were buried on the property of the establishment. *Planetary Energy: Mercury. Elemental Energies: Air, Earth. Astrological Signs: Gemini, Virgo.*

FEVERFEW *(Tranacetum parthenium).* Along with eucalyptus, feverfew is another cold and flu magickal favorite for those conjuring bags and for around your healing candles of pink or green. The herb can also be added to magick involving travel or protection for those who are employed in some type of hazardous duty. Empower when the Moon is in Cancer to keep "accident" energy out of the home, and hang in a small bag above the most dangerous places in the household: bathroom and kitchen. Grind together with hyssop, juniper berries, comfrey, and rosemary to prevent accidents on the road or on the job. *Planetary Energy: Moon. Elemental Energy: Water. Astrological Energy: Cancer.*

one
two
three
four
five

186

FLAX SEED *(Linum usitatissimum)*. Also called linseed. The fibers from flax are woven into linen, creating a strong, durable material. Linen appears in ancient history, including Egyptian and Teuton practice and legend. Egyptians wrapped their mummies in linen, whereas Teutonic practice attributed the plant to a specific goddess, Hulda (Dame Holda), who supposedly taught humans to grow, cultivate, harvest, spin, and weave the flax fibers (when she wasn't busy commanding hounds and ghosts). Although she is referenced with harvest energy, winter is her primary seasonal power and the snowflake is her emblem. From biblical references to a mention in the *Odyssey*, flax has a long and durable history, including as an additive in some breads and in the creation of ropes, strings, fishnets, sails, and car wax. I first learned about flax seed not through clothing or food but in its use in oil painting as an additive to keep the paint smooth and pliable when applying to canvas. The odor of linseed oil takes me back to childhood when my father taught me how to use the oil painting medium. In magick, flax seed has a compendium of uses, including increasing monetary gain, adding durability to a spell, protection, and healing. A most interesting use, however, comes from an urban legend that people have drowned in vats of flax seed because the seeds are so slippery. If you need to skinny out of a problem that you did not create, softly rub the flax seeds in your hands, visualizing yourself slipping out of the noose. Conversely, if you need to keep a wicked person busy, write his or her name on a piece of paper and bury it in a small jar of flax seed. Carry the jar off your property and bury it. This is not intended to harm, just to keep the individual from further harassing you. Add a layer of cat's claw and black pepper for extremely difficult cases. For monetary difficulties (and especially to bring food into the home), mix flax seed and alfalfa in a conjuring bag. Place it by the

one
two
three
four
five

187

stove and conjure for prosperity in hearth and home. Empower as you bake a loaf of bread, allowing the aroma to act as a trigger during the magickal process. If you are just learning magick and are having difficulty warding your home from unwanted visitors, combine flax seed with black pepper and angelica in a black bag and hang it near the most-used door. (Works for experienced practitioners as well.) To protect your vehicle from theft, mix flax seed, juniper berries, and holly or rue into a charm or talisman and place inside the car or truck. *Planetary Energy: Mercury. Elemental Energies: Air, Earth. Astrological Signs: Gemini, Virgo.*

one

two

three

four

five

❖

188

FRANKINCENSE TEARS RESIN *(Boswellia cateri)*. Native to Ethiopia. "Rich" is the only way to describe the aroma of frankincense. Eggshell in color with a yellowish tint, this resin has been used in a variety of cultures for honoring deity and the purification of a sacred area. A calming scent, especially when mixed with ceremonial sage or lavender, it is therefore ideal for meditation and vision questing. Used often in money spells or workings where financial wizardry is a must. *Planetary Energy: Sun. Elemental Energy: Fire. Astrological Sign: Leo.*

GALANGAL ROOT *(Alpine galanga)*. Galangal, buckthorn, celandine, and brown sugar combine to make the ultimate magickal mix for any legal difficulty. Light a brown candle on one side and a red on the other (some prefer pink) and you have three-fourths of the standard spell for most legal malfunctions. Galangal, a member of the ginger family, has a spicy aroma and acts as a motivator, sometimes called "Low John the Conquerer" (not to be confused with High John, which is jalop). Mixed with patchouli and red peppers, you have a sure-fire grouping for lust magick (just don't inhale it or your sex life will be temporarily over, unless of course you find puffy, watery eyes and a runny nose attractive). Add to bee pollen to motivate a group of individuals. Use with runes carved on a red candle to jolt loose an otherwise hopelessly stuck situation. *Planetary Energy: Mars. Elemental Energy: Fire. Astrological Signs: Aries, Scorpio (classical).*

GINGER ROOT *(Zingiber officinale).* Another Hoodoo favorite, ginger root, like vervain and hot peppers, is used to speed up the manifestation of a spell or force something that's stuck to let loose, bringing back the natural flow of energy. Works extremely well with Runic War Fetters, as well as magick involving success, gain, and forward thinking. A common ingredient in love magick whether you are trying to heat up a marriage that's gotten a bit cool or add a bit of lust to your current relationship. In candle magick try using this herb with patchouli, bee pollen, or dragon's blood to enhance love, money, and success. If you need a boost in your business, make yourself a "trick" out of red felt, place your petition inside, add a magnet or lodestone, dab with honey, sprinkle with ginger root and red clover, wrap securely, and dab with a business-related magickal oil. Place near the business, then sprinkle the area with red clover water in an effort to lure successful energy into the establishment. *Planetary Energy: Mars. Elemental Energies: Fire, Water. Astrological Signs: Aries, Scorpio (classical).*

GOLDENSEAL *(Hydrastis canadensis).* Eye root (folk name). Medicinally popular at the moment, folk magick references to this herb include second sight and divinatory pursuits, clearing of the mind for better magickal performance, breaking blocks in monetary issues, and assisting one in finding solutions to sticky financial problems (use a gold gris-gris bag for this). Can be used in spells for stress reduction and restful sleep, especially if added to chamomile and lavender (use a blue or purple bag).

one

two

three

four

five

189

As with many herbs, this one functions well in healing magick with a white conjuring bag or poppet. A "guardian" herb, sprinkle goldenseal around candles when asking for assistance from your spirit teacher, guardian angel, or totem animal. *Planetary Energy: Sun. Elemental Energy: Fire. Astrological Sign: Leo.*

one

two

three

four

five

❖

190

GOTU KOLA *(Centella asiatica).* If you are working on something that you would like to last long-term, choose the Waxing Moon in Taurus (see if you can get a fixed sign on the rising and midheaven or at least on the cusp of the house the desire might be attributed to) and add gotu kola to your spellwork. Write your petition on a piece of paper, sprinkle with gotu kola, tie securely shut with a brown ribbon, and nail to the ground to "set" the energies of your request. This herb is also added to conjuring bags for divinatory purposes, in spells for growth (linked with wormwood), and stability in finances. *Planetary Energy: Saturn. Elemental Energies: Earth, Air. Astrological Signs: Capricorn, Aquarius (classical).*

GUM ARABIC. Sometimes called Egyptian gum, this powder is a derivative of the acacia plant. Primarily used as an additive and binding agent, this white powder resin is a main ingredient in magickal inks (including bat's blood ink and dragon's blood ink) and powdered incenses to give the mixture more body. Magickally it is considered an appropriate additive for calling "good spirits" (including the honorable dead), cleansing and purification rites, and visionary work (divination, vision questing, and meditation). Although some people do add this powder to herbal mixtures, I don't recommend it unless you are making herbal incense, as gum arabic "floats" because it is a clingy white powder and coats everything it touches. *Planetary Energy: Mercury. Elemental Energy: Air. Astrological Signs: Libra, Virgo.*

HAWTHORN *(Crataegus sp.)*. A mixture of hawthorn and linden are commonly used in Wiccan handfasting ceremonies to draw love, happiness, and protection into the marriage vow. Hawthorn reminds me of the Pennsylvania Dutch bluebird of happiness because that is this herb's primary focus: all that is joyful, entertaining, and upbeat. Use in spells or rituals to remove sorrow from the home, find a good mate, or guard small children. Put in a gris-gris bag to relieve the grief of those who are left behind in a crossing ritual. Place in a conjuring bag in the room where a person sleeps who cannot seem to get over the death of a pet or loved one. Also considered a ghost-buster herb when mixed with other leaves and resins, including angelica and larkspur, in exorcism spells. *Planetary Energy: Mars. Elemental Energy: Fire. Astrological Signs: Aries, Scorpio.*

one

two

three

four

five

191

HEAL–ALL *(Prunella vulgaris)*. Not to be confused with valerian, which also has the folk name of heal-all and in Hoodoo is called vandal root. Self-heal or heal-all is common in folk herbal remedies for throat ailments. Its many-flowered spikes and hairy bracelets give us the correspondence of the circle of protection, and it is excellent in magick when you are protecting yourself from lies, harmful gossip, and other communicative difficulties. This is a plant that primarily deals with problems people cause through their words and actions—anything from the inconsiderate to the downright malicious. It can help you punch through to the truth or bore through a serious difficulty when light must be shed on the entire situation for clear thought. Used in meditation to open the throat chakra, especially if combined in a gris-gris bag with blue gemstones, such as turquoise or sodalite, or even blue glass beads. This works especially well if you are dealing with low self-esteem or a situation in which people have gossiped against you and your self-worth is at issue. Also excellent to use in healing poppets to assist in keeping up one's spirits through medical difficulties. If someone has been a particular nuisance and you want them to forget you and move on with their life, write their name on a white card. Cut into a circle with the name in the center. Indicate that banishment in a quiet, unassuming way is of immediate necessity. Put the paper in the center of a Spirit Circle. Place a white candle on top. Surround the candle with heal-all mixed with white blitz (see part one). Add copal resin either around the candle or burn it as incense while completing the spellwork. Allow the candle to burn completely. Throw the spell ingredients off your property when the candle has finished burning. This small spell is an additional additive for full rituals involving the banishment of stalkers, abusive partners, or people whom you have grown away from and have tried very nicely to extricate from your life, but they stubbornly won't go. Excellent for that one-time date that keeps calling and never in a million years will you go out with them again. A nice tie-up spell after divorce proceedings, moving out of a house or apartment where the landlord was a nightmare, or a job that became intolerable because of rampant gossip. *Planetary Energy: Mercury. Elemental Energies: Earth, Air. Astrological Signs: Virgo, Libra.*

HIBISCUS FLOWERS *(Hibiscus sabdariffa)*. A popular ingredient in divinatory herbal mixtures, the hibiscus flower is also known as rose mallow and is of the mallow family. Found in swampy areas, it is no surprise that its magickal correspondences include clairvoyance, divination, psychic development, tranquility, and prophecy. Unfortunately, dried hibiscus does not have the vibrant color or lovely scent of the fresh flowers. Sometimes a magickal oil relating to the spell's purpose is blended with these sturdy petals before use in divination or ritual. Some

one

two

three

four

five

❖

192

practitioners believe that adding a moonstone to the mixture increases the potency. Mix with lavender and chamomile for peaceful sleep, and with bethroot and patchouli for any love spell. Used in many potpourri blends, not for the scent but for the color and texture. Steep in hot water, allow water to cool, and sprinkle in divination area and on divination table and tools. Place dried flowers in the light of a full moon for additional divinatory energy. Also used in spells where determination is vital. *Planetary Energy: Moon. Elemental Energy: Water. Astrological Sign: Cancer.*

one

two

three

four

five

HONEYSUCKLE FLOWERS *(Fuchsia triphylla)*. If you are trying to find a new job or get a raise, the mixture of honeysuckle, devil's shoestring, galangal, and gotu kola can add great oomph to your spellwork. In magick, the trailing vines of this plant guide the way for things to happen and the sweet antiseptic nectar of the flower entices the flow of positive energy. Use in all manner of money magick—general prosperity, building wealth, gaining new customers (and keeping old ones), and financial planning. Mix with bee pollen if you are building a business that includes hiring employees or subcontractors. Place in a jar with alfalfa, gold glitter, and coins if you are having a rough financial patch within the home and paying bills and eating at the same time is a questionable matter. Also used in spells for luck and psychism (which is probably attributed to the classical astrological correspondence). *Planetary Energy: Jupiter. Elemental Energy: Fire. Astrological Signs: Sagittarius, Pisces (classical).*

HOPS *(Humulus lupulus)*. Primarily used as a cleanser, a little bit of hops goes a long way; it has a strong, pungent aroma. Mix with lavender and stuff a pillow for restful sleep, especially if you've been experiencing nightmares or have found it difficult to drift off into dreamland. Add to healing sachets, incenses, powders, gris-gris bags, and poppets. Mix with sea salt and dried garlic and place under the bed to remove negativity from a sickroom. *Planetary Energy: Mercury. Elemental Energy: Air. Astrological Signs: Gemini, Virgo.*

one

two

three

four

five

❖

194

HOREHOUND *(Marrubium vulgare).* Excellent poppet and pillow-stuffing herb—light and fluffy. Sometimes called Eye of the Star or Horus (after the Egyptian deity). Used in protective, healing, and mental pursuits. Given as an offering to Egyptian deities in general. Place in a bowl of clear water with rose petals, rosemary, and a quartz crystal to cleanse the vibrations of a room. Sprinkle infusion of same on divination table between customers to keep the air free from negativity. *Planetary Energy: Mercury. Elemental Energy: Air. Astrological Signs: Gemini, Virgo.*

HYSSOP *(Hyssopus officinalis).* From the mint family, hyssop is one of my favorite herbs. I like the mild, camphorlike odor, especially when mixed with lavender and chamomile—you know you have an herbal blend with a bit of magickal punch! To me, the herb does not have an unpleasant smell—I think of "clean" and use it in many healing spells. Mentioned in ancient texts as an herb used in purification ceremonies and the cleansing of sacred temples by the Hebrews, Greeks, and Romans (although the etymologists of today are not sure if the modern hyssop is the same as the ancient plant). During medieval times it was strewn in the home and other buildings to dispel sickness and unpleasant odors. Some magickal individuals blend thyme, hyssop, and rosemary for ritual baths. These same three herbs are sometimes steeped in hot spring water, then the liquid is cooled for addition to holy water formulas. If you have difficulty expressing your feelings due to self-doubt or self-imposed limitations, carry a conjuring bag with hyssop, black cohosh, and mullein. This herb is an excellent inclusion in any healing poppet or gris-gris bag! *Planetary Energy: Jupiter. Elemental Energy: Fire. Astrological Sign: Sagittarius.*

IRISH MOSS FLAKES *(Chondrus crispus).* Definitely a fragrance from the bog. One of the few herbs associated with weather magick, its correspondences also cover luck, the flow of money, and protecting your financial interests. Works well with red clover in regard to finances and with bladderwrack and pansy/violet for weather magick. Use to create a "trick" or a "toby" (root worker slang for a small felt packet hand-stitched and stuffed with interesting items) to place under the rug (though if you have pets, this is a bad idea—hang from a nail atop the door frame instead). The spongy consistency makes this a great herb for stuffing money poppets, money jars, and conjuring bags. I use it for fast cash and money mixes. *Planetary Energy: Moon. Elemental Energy: Water. Astrological Sign: Cancer.*

JASMINE FLOWERS *(Jasminium officinale).* Ah, the heady energy of love! Jasmine's specialty in the magickal herbal department is intoxication—no, not the bottle-tipping type, the walking-on-water euphoria! Dried jasmine, however, does not carry much of a scent and you may wish to add a few drops of your favorite compelling magickal oil to your gris-gris bag or potpourri. Like the goddess Venus, jasmine flowers pack a mighty punch, so use sparingly. Excellent for use in enchantments wherein you are working to dispel sadness. Great for general work of happiness and love. Ruled by the Moon, jasmine can assist with rituals for the manifestation of material objects, wealth, and prosperity. Used in handfasting herbal mixes and some meditation blends. However, and please read this carefully, if you have many allergies (or any at all), be careful with

one

two

three

four

five

195

jasmine. There are some individuals that just can't tolerate this plant, which is why I haven't recommended any to-go-withs for spellworking purposes. Unfortunately, jasmine flowers (like many others, including honeysuckle and magnolia) do not hold the plant's powerful, heady scent. An essential oil or fragrance would need to be added if you want both the power of the plant itself and the aromatic sensation. Just remember, jasmine is one of those herbs where a little bit goes a long way. *Planetary Energy: Moon. Elemental Energy: Water. Astrological Sign: Cancer.*

one

two

three

four

five

✥

JUNIPER BERRIES *(Juniperus communis).* Surprisingly enough, juniper is the primary flavoring in gin, which is the origin of the plant's name *jenever* (Dutch). Add juniper berries to any spell designed to ward against theft, whether you are protecting your automobile or something less physical, like an idea or job proposal. Extremely protective, medieval correspondences include warding against attacks from wild beasts (in this day psychodramas by humans would apply) and magickally guarding against sickness and accidents, ghosts and rabid bosses. In Hoodoo conjurations, juniper berries are associated with luck in love and are often combined with damiana. Mix with rosebuds or petals to ensure a secret is kept. Use with coltsfoot and horehound for animal magick. *Planetary Energy: Sun. Elemental Energy: Fire. Astrological Sign: Leo.*

KAVA KAVA *(Piper methysticum).* If it is a twist of Hawaiian magick you'd like to add to your enchantments, kava kava may be just the right ingredient in that very special spell! Sometimes called ava root (first woman), this Saturnian herb is said to provide visions, luck, and protection to the bearer. Use in divinatory mixes with uva ursi, damiana, and wormwood for learning to move beyond the veil. If luck is on your mind, a combination of kava kava, orange peel, and fava beans rolled in cotton and offered to the spirits is said to bring good luck and fortune to the wish-maker. *Planetary Energy: Saturn. Elemental Energy: Earth. Astrological Sign: Capricorn.*

LARKSPUR *(Consolida).* Scorpion Eater. If you don't want to see ghosties and things that go bump in the night, use larkspur; conversely, if your goal in life is to be a ghost-watcher, don't carry this vibrantly attractive herb. Legend has it that larkspur keeps away things that like to jab or bite, physically and spiritually; therefore, you'll find these lovely flowers in conjuring bags designed to stop gossip and destroy stinging words, thoughts, and deeds. A deep blue-purple, larkspur adds a bit of zest to any magickal herbal mix (herbs can look so boring all jumbled together). Mix with lavender, chamomile, rose petals, and sunflower petals for business success. If you have a particular area of the house that seems to be a portal for someplace else, hang a muslin bag of larkspur there to deter anything from wandering through. If you have a child that isn't ready to "see things," a nice sachet tucked under the bed containing larkspur certainly helped in our home. Mix larkspur with lavender and rosemary if troubled by nightmares, and sew into an herbal pillow to place under your regular pillow. Mound larkspur on top of a picture of someone who is saying hateful things about you and cover with a heavy stone—river rock or creek stone will do. Place a tiger-eye stone on top so that they will be weighted down by their own words (and eventually caught). Surround a blue candle with larkspur during meditation and vision questing for extra astral security. *Planetary Energy: Pluto. Elemental Energy: Water. Astrological Sign: Scorpio (like unto like).*

one

two

three

four

five

197

LAVENDER BUDS *(Lavandula angustifolia)*. Lavender smells great, the energy is fantastic, it has a variety of magickal uses as well as practical ones, and it is a firm choice for protecting children, removing sorrow, and providing comfort in a crossing ritual of a person or pet. Works well with every type of deity energy because of its versatility. Practically, it is an herb that can be placed around the home to keep away fleas and relieve stress. Magickally it corresponds to love, peaceful sleep, long life, happiness, and, of course, purification. Sometimes called elf leaf, historically it was worn to ward off spousal abuse as well as to entice the male gender. Used in herbal baths, candles, and simmering potpourri, it is the number-one herb for anti-stress, anti-nightmare, and peaceful sleep. Excellent for stuffing poppets and dream pillows. *Planetary Energy: Mercury. Elemental Energy: Air. Astrological Sign: Gemini.*

LEMONGRASS *(Cymbopogon citratus)*. Excellent cleansing herb mixed with hyssop and lemon verbena. Used in protective sachets, gris-gris bags, and poppets to ward from danger and negativity. Combine with uva ursi, eyebright, and damiana around a blue candle for a ritual to increase psychic awareness or carry this mixture in a gris-gris bag along with a tiger-eye gemstone if you plan to divine in public. *Planetary Energy: Mercury. Elemental Energy: Air. Astrological Sign: Gemini.*

LEMON VERBENA *(Aloysia triphylla)*. Highly aromatic. *Rodale's Illustrated Encyclopedia of Herbs* tells us that lemon verbena "charmed" the Spanish explorers during their conquests; commercially it is used in body splashes, perfumes, and herbal baths. A plant with a variety of applications, it has been used as a body rub, in potpourri, a tea, and added to culinary pursuits (like chicken and vegetable marinades, dressings and other delights). Magickally it is perfect for aura-cleansing mixes, especially when added to lavender and rosemary. Add to your holy water when asperging sacred space. Some feel that the scent is much like patchouli in drawing love interests to you, and therefore you will find these scented leaves in various love spells and poppets. A light mixture of patchouli and lemon verbena can be added to muslin conjuring bags carried in the pocket to enhance your appeal. Excellent for healing mixes, add lemon verbena to other healing correspondence herbs such as eucalyptus, mint, pine, wintergreen, and willow. Use lemon verbena in herbal mixes designed for cold and flu season. Not only does it smell wonderful, the properties of the herb helps to cleanse the aura of the room. Don't miss putting this aromatic herb in your magickal cabinet! *Planetary Energy: Mercury. Elemental Energies: Earth, Air. Astrological Signs: Virgo, Libra.*

one

two

three

four

five

✣

199

LINDEN *(Tilia europea)*. I wasn't familiar with this herb until I started my Hoodoo training. It is one of the few herbs associated with luck and protecting one's ability to draw good fortune to the household. Mixed with dried citrus peels, the blend is a great magickal purifier during household cleansing rites. Linden is also used in sleep sachets when lilac, chamomile, and lavender are added. Functions as an ingredient in anti-nightmare spells where restful sleep and protection must be combined; also found in handfasting and marriage magick. *Planetary Energy: Jupiter. Elemental Energy: Fire. Astrological Sign: Sagittarius.*

LOBELIA *(Lobelia inflata)*. Whether you are working with Pennsylvania Dutch Pow-Wow magick, Hoodoo, or are just way into folk magick, lobelia is an all-time favorite of many practitioners. Its primary use is to stop a blabbermouth. Mix with plantain, slippery elm, and wormwood, then place in a poppet of your own design. Hang it from a tree so that the individual will get "caught up" in his or her own lies. A bit more pricy than most magickal herbs (though not the most expensive), lobelia falls under the auspices of the dark goddesses in its ability to halt the blackest of tempests (real or astral) and stop the emotional turmoil of a stormy relationship. Another one of those herbs considered by the FDA to be unhealthy for human consumption. *Planetary Energy: Saturn. Elemental Energies: Earth, Air. Astrological Signs: Capricorn, Aquarius (classical).*

MANDRAKE *(Mandragora officinarum)*. Called Hexenkraut (Witch's wort) in the Middle Ages in Germany, those who kept a mandrake root in their homes were thought to derive information of past and future through hidden and obscure connections to the spirit world. There are three different types of mandrake— the American May apple, the European mandrake (popularized by a Harry Potter scene), and Hecate's mandrake, which is belladonna (atropa or garden nightshade). Although all three are related, the last two, European mandrake and belladonna, are magickally considered polar opposites—the first associated with male energy and the second with feminine power and mystique. All three types of mandrake (difficult to procure unless wildcrafted by the Witch) are used in spells when the total destruction and banishment of an energy is necessary. From spiraling root to white flower, in Greek writings, the plant symbolized the alchemical manifestation of divine energy. Occasionally used in love spells. *Planetary Energy: Mercury. Elemental Energy: Air. Astrological Sign: Gemini.*

MISTLETOE *(Phoradendron flavescens)*. This is one of my all-time favorite herbs for magick—more power, more strength, more gusto for your mojo! For gain and good luck, success and power, a little bit of mistletoe goes a long way in any working.

one

two

three

four

five

200

In the past, we've used it for money, banishing stalkers, healing, protection, and ritual for deity honor. Use in financial magick when you are concentrating on debt reduction. *Planetary Energy: Sun. Elemental Energy: Fire. Astrological Sign: Aries.*

MOONFLOWER *(Ipomoea alba).* A fast-growing, soft-stemmed, evergreen perennial whose vines can grow up to twenty feet! (Considered an annual in northern climes.) With the right conditions, the heart-shaped leaves can span eight to ten inches in width and are perfect for spells in which you wish to hold on to your money in a positive way. Using the large leaf like a piece of cloth, place a tonka bean, a dollar bill, and a bit of yellow dock root in the center; gently fold it shut and tie with golden thread. Bury it at the front door of your home or business establishment. Under a full moon, place offerings to the Goddess on one of the large, heart-shaped leaves with a crystal in the center when requesting personal empowerment. The crowning glory and the unique aspect of this plant are large pure-white flowers that bloom at dusk and remain open throughout the night. The flower lasts only one day, but the plant produces many blooms from midsummer to first frost. Use these for night magick and purification rituals. The blossom, right before opening, is large and oval, with the petals swirling in a spiral to the tip. Perfect for a ritual garden trellis, as it climbs on its own and provides dense privacy if several plants are close to one another. The very nature of the moonflower makes this plant ideal for binding and sealing magick as the vine shoots literally reach out to capture anything. These vines climb up and along posts, fences, even vertical wires. Once the vine finger touches an object, the vine will naturally curl around it in about twenty-four hours. Best used as a living plant, the dried leaves and flowers can also be employed in conjuring and gris-gris bags, especially if you are trying to

one

two

three

four

five

201

diminish illness or are bracketing a diet with magickal practices. If you have a problem person in your life and you wish to entrap them in their own negativity, take their picture or write their name on a piece of paper, roll the paper away from you in a small tube, tie shut with black thread or seal with wax; wrap the living finger of the plant around the paper and tie with another string; the paper is now securely on the vine. From one moon to the next, the person is often gone from your life. Note that the moonflower is poisonous. *Planetary Energy: Moon. Elemental Energy: Water. Astrological Sign: Cancer.*

one

two

three

four

five

❖

MOTHERWORT *(Leonurus cardiaca)*. The "woman's herb" is used primarily in magick for a safe delivery in childbirth rituals and conjuring bags. From the mint family, the plant has "teeth" on the lobes (the protective energy of a mother roused to defense) and the flowers contain a pink whorl, signifying the spiral of birth and death and the manifestation of the child into this plane of existence. For birthing, embroider the Birca rune (ᛒ) on the conjuring bag and add this herb and a lock of hair from each (healthy) member of the family (or friends in your magick circle). Other protective herbs can be added as well. Use in magick to protect children, animals, the physically or mentally challenged, or the emotionally weak. Also used in dream magick; place in a sachet with lavender and chamomile for under your pillow. *Planetary Energy: Venus. Elemental Energy: Earth. Astrological Sign: Taurus.*

MUGWORT *(Artemisia vulgaris)*. A close relative of wormwood, mugwort figures prominently in Middle Age legend as a protector against evil manifestations. Definitely a witchy favorite, probably because of its interesting name, today you will find mugwort often added to a variety of holistic herbal baths. Mugwort is also popular in Hoodoo magick because it guards against all poisons—of the body, mind, or spirit (including hateful critics and gossipy idiots). Sometimes called the herb of Artemis, it is associated with the energy, wisdom, and strength of the bear totem. It has several uses in magick, including healing, protection, and strengthening intuition and psychic pursuits. Mixed with other scrying herbs, conjuring bags can be placed with your divination tools to keep them fresh. Steep in hot water along with eyebright to cleanse crystals and moonstones. Added to hawthorn in spells, it is used to call fertile energies to both people and pets. A prime favorite in exorcism spells as well (which is how I first learned to use it) and for stuffing dream pillows to ward off nightmares. Can also be used to stimulate energy patterns in magickal work, enhance the regularity of energy, and "sweat" the truth out in a nasty situation. *Planetary Energy: Venus. Elemental Energy: Earth. Astrological Sign: Taurus.*

one

two

three

four

five

❖

203

MULLEIN *(Verbascum thapsus).* If you feel some wild human has set you for his or her prey, mullein is your choice of herbal shield! Used for warding, health matters, love, divinatory pursuits, banishment, and even fortitude, this all-purpose herb is great to have in your magickal cupboard. Place in a gris-gris bag with rue and angelica dotted with clove oil to protect the home or business establishment. Mix with damiana, uva ursi, eyebright, wormwood, and spearmint for spells involving psychism and mental clarity (but do *not* ingest the mixture). *Planetary Energy: Saturn. Elemental Energy: Earth. Astrological Signs: Aquarius, Capricorn.*

MYRRH GUM *(Commiphora molmol).* The action resin that is popular as a magickal blending vehicle, much like a bindrune where various energies are bound together in one sigil. Here, myrrh binds the energies of plants and resins for a more seamless magickal working. Along with its binding properties, myrrh also has healing associations and has been used in toothpastes and mouthwashes. Mix with sandalwood and burn on charcoal brick specifically made for incenses during Reiki or Pow-Wow treatments, or when working healing spells. Can be added to love magick herbal mixtures, especially for money and love, and is combined with copal to break spells. *Planetary Energy: Mars. Elemental Energy: Fire. Astrological Signs: Aries, Scorpio.*

NETTLE *(Urtica diocia).* Easy to obtain during the summer months, nettles are often the prime ingredient when dealing with the nastier aspects of human behavior; however, if you choose to gather it yourself, use gloves as the teeny thorns will work their way under your skin and you will be more than miserable. Often depicted in paintings of Witches in the Middle Ages, associating the nature of the plant to the wilderness and the ability to overrun the mind. Added to other herbs of exorcism, it is often scattered in the footsteps of an undesirable individual whom you desperately need to vacate a building or your life in general. Also used in karmic return spells, especially in combination with graveyard dirt and coffin nails (the nails are to seal the spell). Added to mugwort and elder, this trinity of herbs aids in hefty spell-breaking magick. Associated most often with Hecate, dark goddesses in general seem to work quite well with this plant. Scatter around a black skull candle or figure candle to exorcise an unwanted individual or bad habit. A favorite of the Egyptian goddess Selkhet, the Scorpion Queen. In Pow-Wow magick the herb is mixed with hot pepper and rubbed into the underwear of a cheating husband, then burned in a cauldron during divorce proceedings to ensure that the truth of his infidelity becomes known.

one

two

three

four

five

204

Throw in a tiger-eye gem and you'll have a bonanza of information. *Planetary Energy: Mars. Elemental Energy: Fire. Astrological Signs: Aries, Scorpio.*

OAK MOSS *(Evernia prunastri)*. In magick as well as potpourri recipes, oak moss is considered a fixative. From a magickal perspective the moss is used to seal a spell. In potpourri mixes the moss helps to hold the scent for a longer-lasting blend. Oak moss is also employed in binding spells and, since it is nice and fluffy, to stuff healing poppets in hopes of not only holding the spell in place for as long as possible but also to provide superior strength to the individual in need. Herbal mixtures for courage commonly use oak moss as a primary ingredient. For added strength, empower when the Moon is in a fixed astrological sign: Scorpio, Aquarius, Leo, or Taurus. *Planetary Energy: Venus. Elemental Energy: Earth. Astrological Sign: Taurus.*

ORRIS ROOT *(Iris florentina)*. Orris root is a "commanding" herb and is used by magickal practitioners in various rites involving the elements, protection, stopping gossip (use with plantain and gag root [lobelia]), exorcism, and divination. Orris is an herbal fixative employed to hold the scent of other herbs in gris-gris bags, dream pillows, potpourri, and loose incense. Orris is actually the rhizome of the Florentine iris. Unlike many herbs, orris root actually gets better as it grows older, taking on its own particular odor if aged for at least two years (discovered by the Egyptians). It is commercially used in blends that attempt to mimic violets. Some Hoodoo practitioners add this root to spells and conjure bags for love, citing its ability to attract "of a like mind," and it is the primary ingredient in many love-drawing powders. *Planetary Energy: Venus. Elemental Energies: Air, Earth. Astrological Signs: Libra, Taurus.*

one

two

three

four

five

205

one

two

three

four

five

✧

206

PANSY *(Viola)*. If you want to make it rain or let it snow, then the violet (pansy) is the magickal herb for you! Conversely, if you want the precipitation to stop, add to bladderwrack, put it in the palm of your hand, and cast it in a complete circle, calling the four winds to cease and desist. Hey, it works for me. Sometimes called Johnny Jump-Ups or Kiss Me Over the Garden Gate, the pansy is employed in a variety of love magick. Mix with passion flower and roses, add a bit of magickal attraction oil, and you have a recipe to use in spells to gain friends and positive business associates. Add a bit of patchouli and ginger to this mix and dot a conjuring bag with red pepper for a hotter relationship. Divination is another pursuit of the magickal pansy, and therefore you will find it in various grimoires added to the likes of damiana, uva ursa, orris root, and wormwood. If you desperately need someone to tell the truth, add pansy to a poppet that includes a taglock of that person (or their name), a tiger-eye gemstone, a piece of frankincense or copal resin for the heart, and a magnet. Tie the poppet to a drum and trance the heartbeat for at least fifteen minutes, adding your own word charm as appropriate. You should have the truth shortly. *Planetary Energy: Venus. Elemental Energies: Earth, Air. Astrological Signs: Libra, Taurus.*

PASSION FLOWER *(Passiflora incarnata)*. Herb of creativity. This is a great herb to add to spellwork when you are trying to make new friends, especially if you have just moved from a different location or to a new job. Combined with lavender and chamomile, it makes a nice sleep sachet. If you need to win some sort of popularity contest for a good cause, add this herb to your enchantments. Excellent herb for writers and poets. Mix with basil and hawthorn to quell arguments in the home or on the job. If you are negotiating a big contract and some of the participants just can't keep their mouths off of each other, add this herb to your gris-gris bag along with red clover and uva ursi. *Planetary Energy: Venus. Elemental Energy: Air. Astrological Sign: Libra.*

PATCHOULI *(Pogostemon cablin)*. There are several "power-house" herbs in medieval magickal correspondences and patchouli is definitely one of them. It has an enticing, musky scent, a sort of deep autumn aroma with a floral touch. Called "graveyard dust" by some, this herb has been used as an exorcism ingredient, to help develop psychism and meditation abilities, for clear sight in divination, to break spells (your own and others), entice the opposite sex, and increase the power of any magickal working. *Planetary Energy: Saturn. Elemental Energy: Earth. Astrological Signs: Capricorn, Aquarius (classical).*

PENNYROYAL *(Mentha puleguim)*. An herb of Demeter, this is one of the bug removers of the herbal kingdom. Coupled with lavender in felt packets and tucked into furniture, it has been known to kill fleas. Mix with chamomile and a lodestone to draw money. Add to holy basil to clear the air after an argument. Used in warding, home happiness, and rituals for self-confidence. The FDA indicates this herb is harmful if taken internally. *Planetary Energy: Mars. Elemental Energy: Fire. Astrological Sign: Mars.*

PEPPER, WHITE. Used in a variety of Hoodoo spells to set some action into the working. Add to all white/off-white action herbs such as calamus, orris root, white beans, and ginger for a thrust of power! *Planetary Energy: Mars. Elemental Energy: Fire. Astrological Sign: Mars.*

one
two
three
four
five

207

PEPPERMINT LEAF *(Mentha piperita)*. If it is mental magick you have in mind, ease in completion of a project, the desire for money, healing, restful sleep, psychic endeavors, or clearing the air of negativity—peppermint just might do the trick! Cleanse the front door of your business with an infusion of peppermint and chamomile to increase business. To make the spell move quickly, try mixing peppermint, vervain, and ginger, sprinkling around a double-action or vervain herbal candle. *Planetary Energy: Mercury. Elemental Energy: Air. Astrological Sign: Gemini.*

PLANTAIN *(Plantago major)*. Plantain is best known for its ability to heal the wounds caused by stinging words in the magickal world or those irritating zaps from half-baked magicians; however, in mundane society, there is nothing better than drawing out a bee sting when there ain't nothin' around. *Out on the baseball field the child screams and the bee zooms away. Crush plantain and apply. Takes the sting out. Witch to the rescue.* Used as a primary ingredient in stop-gossip spells along with slippery elm and lobelia. Combine with calamus to protect your vehicle and ease the weariness of a long day when you know you must go on. Oh, and you'll love this one—certain varieties of plantain are called "pussy-toes" (now you've learned something new for today), which is the most common variety in our area and therefore the plant is appropriate for all manner of feline, catlike magick. This isn't so far off, as legend has it that plantain was used to scare off snakes—therefore, if you have a "snake in the grass" on the job, you might want to extend your claws and carry a little plantain with you. *Planetary Energy: Venus. Elemental Energy: Earth. Astrological Sign: Taurus.*

QUEEN OF THE MEADOW *(Eupatorium purpureum)*. Use for offerings to the Goddess and protection of children and women, especially during childbirth or when under attack of some

one

two

three

four

five

✦

208

kind. An herb of command, use for warding, healing, and working on one's self-image. Mix with angel wings and lavender to make wishes outdoors. *Planetary Energy: Sun. Elemental Energy: Fire. Astrological Sign: Leo.*

RED CLOVER *(Trifolium pratense).* There is nothing prettier than looking out across a field filled with the magick of red clover on a warm summer's day. This is another herb that has a variety of correspondences from finding treasure, protecting individuals in human services (armed forces, police, emergency medical, firefighters, etc.), and dealing with money troubles. Red clover water helps with financial arrangements of all types. In magickal work it is used to banish astral nasties (mix with larkspur) and remove blocks from financial concerns. Can also be employed in love and spells of passion. A mixture of cinquefoil, holy basil, and red clover scattered around a white candle does wonders in any magick centered on protecting your family business (financial or otherwise) and allowing your personal concerns to flourish. *Planetary Energy: Mercury. Elemental Energy: Air. Astrological Signs: Libra, Virgo.*

ROSEBUDS AND PETALS *(Rosa canina).* Did you ever open your mouth and vent to a friend and then wish to whatever runs the universe that you'd kept your fool tongue tied to the roof of your mouth? Rosebuds aren't just for love—they're for keeping secrets, too. Or did someone tell you something that you are just dying to unload, but you know that if you do you will lose that friend forever? Whip out the rosebuds and start working the magick on your loose lips. Roses are often added to Craft and Druid initiation rituals to remind the student of their promise to guard the secrets of the group to which they now belong. Use with oak moss and orris root to keep your magickal work secret. Secrets aside, the general consensus of

one

two

three

four

five

209

the general population relates the rose to the magick (and poetry) of love. Mix with hawthorn and linden to keep your present relationship firm. Use in spells to attract new friends or a new pet. Add to any spell where you wish to do your working centered in love, whether it be personal or universal—healing, protection, and even banishment. *Planetary Energies: Venus, Moon. Elemental Energy: Water. Astrological Sign: Cancer.*

ROSEMARY *(Rosmarinus officinalis)*. Nature's cleanser! A popular addition to house-cleansing spells and rituals as well as love rites and enchantments. Combine with lemongrass to remove the poison from a situation. Mix with lavender, blessed thistle, dried garlic, and hops for a healing poppet. Combine with patchouli, rose petals, and yohimbe to draw passion. Also considered a sleep aid, it can be mixed with peppermint or spearmint for an aromatic catalyst for focused mental energy. *Planetary Energy: Sun. Elemental Energy: Fire. Astrological Sign: Leo.*

RUE *(Ruta graveolens)*. Rue is a witchy favorite when it comes to protecting home, family, and property. Used to banish unwanted neighbors, unwanted in-laws, and astral nasties, it is usually placed in a conjuring bag and hung above all entrances to the home or apartment. A favorite of the goddesses Diana and Aradia, both who function in a protective and defensive capacity for the good of the magickal individual, this plant has been employed for a compendium of magick, including removing headaches, adding to healing poppets, and candle magick, and even taking the blindness from the love-struck so that common sense can prevail. A highly popular addition to most hex-breaking spells. Considered a clearing herb, it can be included in household cleansing rituals and karma spells when

one

two

three

four

five

✦

210

what was sent to you is kindly handed back—forthwith! *Planetary Energy: Saturn. Elemental Energy: Earth. Astrological Sign: Capricorn.*

SAFFLOWER PETALS *(Carthamus tinctorius).* Boldly colored, this deep, autumn-orange flower has a long and veritable history when it comes to magickal applications as well as mundane ones. In ancient Egypt safflowers were used as a prime source of cooking oil, dye for food and clothing, and, of course, decorative arrangements for gifts to the gods. Depending upon the culture, the flower was dedicated to the Goddess; promoted love, happiness, and healing; had the power to raise the winds (use with bladderwrack); and gave strength to the practitioner. Combine with damiana and eyebright for increased psychic abilities, bee pollen to command a group of people, or angelica to break a hex. If you want your business to grow, mix with galangal, ginger, and sassafras, and include one tonka bean in the conjuring bag. Add gold glitter and a lodestone (or magnet) to money bags, purses, and wallets. Excellent for any success-related work. Use with gold candles for money, red for action and lust, orange for employment and work-related enchantments, and white or yellow for general success. *Planetary Energy: Sun. Elemental Energy: Fire. Astrological Sign: Leo.*

SAGE, WHITE CEREMONIAL *(Salvia apina).* Most commonly used for incense to cleanse, consecrate, and empower in all manner of magickal applications. It is a highly aromatic stress reliever and aura cleanser. Mix with angel wings and lavender and burn in a cauldron for wishes and wisdom. Add to spells for the health and welfare of senior citizens. *Planetary Energy: Jupiter. Elemental Energies: Fire, Air. Astrological Signs: Sagittarius, Pisces (classical).*

one
two
three
four
five

211

SANDALWOOD, RED CHIPS *(Pterocarpus santalum).* When we experienced a shortage of white sandalwood in the mid 1990s, good old red came to the rescue! Red carries the same magickal connotations as white, but with a bit more punch due to its color; although fragrant, it is not as strong aromatically as the white. Rich and exotic, fragrant woods such as sandalwood, cedar, and evergreen are a favorite for outdoor rituals, needfires, bonfires, and cauldron mixtures. Sandalwood blends extremely well with other herbs, making it the popular choice for homemade incense bases. Magickally, sandalwood (red or yellow) promotes harmony and is a conduit to higher energy vibrations. Extremely versatile, sandalwood powder or chips can be burned during the "big five": money, health, love, protection, and "other" spellworkings. Mix with dragon's blood resin for more power in thurible incense. Add this same mixture to rosebuds and patchouli for a simmering love cauldron. Combine with ginger, galangal, and pink peppercorns for a super-fast action blend! *Planetary Energy: Jupiter. Elemental Energies: Fire, Water. Astrological Signs: Sagittarius, Pisces (classical).*

SANDALWOOD, WHITE. Aromatic. The essential oil and the herb itself are associated with purity and wealth. *Planetary Energy: Jupiter. Elemental Energies: Fire, Water. Astrological Signs: Sagittarius, Pisces (classical).* SEE ALSO Sandalwood, Red Chips.

SARSAPARILLA ROOT *(Smilax ornata). Money, money, money* is the best-known magickal theme for this particular sweet-smelling herb. Used to flavor a variety of beverages, sarsaparilla mixed with aromatic cinnamon, sandalwood, bayberry, frankincense, and myrrh makes a great cauldron herbal mix to increase monetary benefits coming into the home. Excellent for inclusion in a naturally scented magickal potpourri or sachet. *Planetary Energy: Jupiter. Elemental Energies: Fire, Water. Astrological Signs: Sagittarius, Pisces (classical).*

one
two
three
four
five

✦

212

SASSAFRAS ROOT *(Sassafras albidium)*. A Hoodoo favorite for money spells, mix with yellow dock root, chamomile, fava beans, and white beans to draw good fortune. *Planetary Energy: Sun. Elemental Energy: Fire. Astrological Sign: Leo.*

SAW PALMETTO BERRIES *(Sarenoa repens)*. Historically used for food and medicinal purposes by indigenous Floridians before the arrival of all those pesky Europeans. In magick, saw palmetto is used in love spells; mix with bloodroot, rose petals, and yohimbe and make yourself a powerful love poppet. *Planetary Energy: Mars. Elemental Energy: Fire. Astrological Sign: Aries.*

one
two
three
four
five

SKULLCAP *(Scutellaria laterifolia)*. Mad Dog (folk name). Here's a witchy favorite. Used in folk magick applications to ward off mad dogs, wild beasties, and things with teeth that go bump in the night, it's also used to ward off rednecks, blowzy women, and the riffraff with the beer breath that just moved in down the street. Surprisingly enough, skullcap is considered an herb of fidelity and is added to conjuring bags with linden and life everlasting (gotu kola), then placed under the marriage bed to keep the spouse from wandering. This is a Dark Goddess herb often added to petitions and ceremonies of honor in her name. *Planetary Energy: Saturn. Elemental Energies: Earth, Air. Astrological Signs: Capricorn, Aquarius (classical).*

SLIPPERY ELM *(Ulmos rubra)*. Primarily used in healing magick; however, mixed with plantain and lemongrass, you've got a fine mixture to work against slander, Internet "flaming," and other nasty energies in the realm of the spoken word and written missives. Use in cauldron fires with sandalwood and frankincense to cleanse a ritual area. *Planetary Energy: Saturn. Elemental Energy: Earth. Astrological Signs: Capricorn, Aquarius (classical).*

SOLOMON'S SEAL ROOT *(Polygonatum).* Used as individual talismans or amulets, or mixed with other herbs for protection from danger, illness, and psychological dysfunction. Sometimes referred to as "The Seal of Our Lady," meaning where this herb touches, grace and protection are afforded. Mix with sandalwood and copal for a protective, natural incense and burn in a suitable cauldron. Use in gris-gris bags to protect your business establishment. *Planetary Energy: Saturn. Elemental Energy: Earth. Astrological Sign: Capricorn.*

one

two

three

four

five

✤

214

SPIKENARD ROOT *(Aralia racemosa).* American spikenard, related to sarsaparilla. Used in marriage and love spells for harmony, potency, and sexual fidelity. Mix with linden and hawthorn and scatter around a white candle for family happiness. Mix with chamomile, frankincense, and mint for a fragrant money-drawing gris-gris bag. Add to heal-all, rosemary, and lavender for a healing poppet. *Planetary Energy: Moon. Elemental Energy: Water. Astrological Sign: Cancer.*

ST. JOHN'S WORT *(Hypericum perforatum).* Added to hawthorn and linden, legend has it that St. John's wort increases the longevity of a marriage. Add to echinacea, eucalyptus, and feverfew in healing magick. Another one of those herbs considered unhealthy for human consumption. Mix with a lock of a loved one's hair to make soldiers, police officers, and firefighters invincible, probably because of its folk medicinal application to wounds. Sprinkle around a statue or picture of any archangel, Michael and Uriel being the most prominent. *Planetary Energy: Sun. Elemental Energy: Fire. Astrological Sign: Leo.*

STONEROOT *(Collinsonia canadesis).* Used to seal a spell or bring pressure to bear on an issue that needs to be resolved. Mix with graveyard dirt and patchouli to create haunting energy until justice is done. Set in clay with the Isa rune (ᛁ) and place in the freezer to cease movement on any issue. *Planetary Energy: Saturn. Elemental Energy: Earth. Astrological Signs: Capricorn, Aquarius (classical).*

TANSY *(Tanacetum vulgare).* One of the most common European strewing herbs (herbs placed on floors to mask unpleasant smells), the tansy flower looks like a tightly packed miniature sun and is very popular in dried flower arrangements, especially in the harvest months. The plant's name in Greek was *athanasia,* which means "immortality"; therefore, if you want a spell to last a good long while (like a baby blessing or any prayer for continued happiness and good fortune), then the tansy is your magickal herb of choice. Southern magickal practitioners add tansy to conjuring bags to keep the law (or the "system") at bay, which is especially useful if you have been unjustly accused. These bags usually include buckthorn aged bark and celandine as well. If you have been slandered through gossip, mix lobelia, tansy, and black peppercorns in a conjuring bag with a tiger-eye gemstone, or scatter around the base of an empowered candle, or create a poppet with a raw potato and stuff with this herbal combination. Write the perpetrator's name on the poppet with indelible ink and bury it off your property. As the potato rots, their words will turn against them. This does not help you in the deep winter, however. If you wish someone to leave you alone permanently, mix flax seed, graveyard dirt, and tansy in a cup covering the person's name. Place it on your windowsill. Leave it there. I had three cups lined up like that for several years. Worked great! Tansy can also be used in money spells that involve work for solid investments or drawing stable, long-term clientele to your business establishment. *Planetary Energy: Venus. Elemental Energies: Air, Earth. Astrological Signs: Libra, Taurus.*

one
two
three
four
five

215

TONKA BEANS. Considered an herbal charm and poisonous if ingested. Thought to operate like an herbal lodestone, drawing your desires to you. You need use only one bean per magickal application. A powerful fast-cash formula mixed on a new moon and scattered around a golden candle includes sunflower, chamomile, snakeroot, marigold, sarsaparilla, vervain, peppercorns, safflower, bergamot, mountain mint, tonka bean, red clover, and allspice. Add a lodestone or a crystal to the mixture if you're desperate, and perform your chosen working on Friday. *Planetary Energy: Venus. Elemental Energy: Earth. Astrological Sign: Taurus.*

one

two

three

four

five

❖

216

UVA URSI *(Arcostaphylos uva-ursi)*. If you are into protecting animals both big and small, add uva ursi to your spellwork; however, this is one of those herbs that is considered undesirable for human consumption by the FDA, so keep it locked in the magickal cabinet. Used also for spells involving psychism, it is never ingested, only scattered around the base of candles or used in poppets and gris-gris bags. Because of its natural capabilities, this herb is considered highly desirable in spells when great protection is needed. As the ruling planet for uva ursi is Saturn, this herb works well in spells to protect your business and financial dealings or to protect you against others who wish to destroy your fame and fortune in relation to your career pursuits. Mix with red clover and carry in a conjuring bag when making business deals when you feel you may be ripped off, or use if a business deal has gone sour and you wish to recoup your losses. This will only work if you have been legitimately cheated. *Planetary Energy: Saturn. Elemental Energy: Earth. Astrological Sign: Capricorn.*

VETIVER (*Vetiveria zizanioides*). Very popular in the magickal community in the 1960s and early '70s. Grimoires written around that time are filled with recipes for its use, especially in incenses and oils because of vetiver's sweet, musky aroma (if you work with herbals often, you'll learn to enjoy the good-smelling ones like this one). An Asiatic grass, the plant has several magickal associations, including commanding energies, bringing good luck and a prosperous fortune, increasing the power of spells (much like dragon's blood or patchouli), enhancing love (tighten matrimonial bonds by using in spellwork to make you more alluring: soak in his or her favorite scent and place in a sock of yours under your bed), and psychic protection (especially when used in conjunction with wormwood, which calls in just about anything). Combine vetiver with juniper berries to prevent theft, with cinquefoil to increase business success, or with boneset to break a hex. *Planetary Energy: Venus. Elemental Energy: Earth. Astrological Sign: Taurus.*

one

two

three

four

five

217

VIOLET. *See* Pansy.

WHITE OAK BARK *(Quercus alba).* Aromatic barks are excellent for use in potpourris and cauldron fires, great additions to your natural incense blends, and wonderfully enhancing to any ritual, especially when combined with resins and burned. Like mistletoe, the oak has numerous magickal correspondences that cover just about every endeavor of enchantment—love, money, health, protection, strength, fertility, luck, spirituality, and potency. From the Druid belief system to the Pow-Wow hex signs, the mighty oak figures prominently in ritualistic practices and designs. Hoodoo also employs the oak. If you magickally bind any item with oak, so the saying goes, it will not be broken in your lifetime, especially if you use red thread in the spell. Brewed oak water is used to aspurge a ritual area and break hexes, and it is believed that the power is doubled if you add mistletoe and oak to any spellworking. Combine mistletoe, oak bark, and bayberry bark for an aromatic, woodsy blend to be burned on New Year's Day to strengthen the family and entice good fortune. Use with cherry bark to pluck up a love spell—add yohimbe for a "hot" night! Blend with chamomile, gold glitter, and honey to increase gain and stabilize finances. *Planetary Energy: Sun. Elemental Energy: Fire. Astrological Sign: Leo.*

WHITE PINE BARK *(Pinus strobus)*. Considered a spiritual cleanser in many magickal applications, pine essential oil, fragrance, bark, boughs, and needles are used to cleanse sacred space, one's aura, or even one's situation. If you've done a blooper in your spellwork and need to reverse what you've set in motion, add pine bark to your herbal mix. If protection is a necessity over the holiday season, mix pine, oak, and mistletoe in a bowl. Empower by adding a few drops of your favorite protection oil. Write the names of your family members on parchment and place in a Mason jar. Cover with the herbal mix. Add a few sprigs of holly on top. Punch holes in the jar lid, then screw it tightly in place. Add a bow and place as a working decorative piece in the home. To hold the scent, include a little orris root or oak moss. If you are very artistic, you can make a jar for each of your covenmates as a Yule present for strength and protection the whole year through. Tip: If you have someone in circle who is a "black hole," place pine boughs around the entire circle area (just be careful of open flames). *Planetary Energy: Saturn. Elemental Energies: Air, Earth. Astrological Signs: Aquarius, Capricorn.*

WHITE WILLOW *(Salix alba)*. One of my favorite goddess-oriented herbs, the white willow is associated with Artemis, Hecate, Ayzian, and the androgynous Mercury. Although delicate in appearance, the willow tree is one of the strongest and most tenacious plants on earth. Its root system will burrow through almost anything to obtain the large amount of water it needs to survive, including puncturing water pipes and drilling through the stone walls of wells. Leaves are used in a variety of spells, including divination (mixed with damiana and uva ursa), protection (mixed with angelica root and rosemary), healing (combined with eucalyptus, myrrh, sandalwood, mugwort, and mint), and love magick (with rose petals). Whole branches can be used for cleansing sacred space, tying Witch's brooms, or as temporary poppets. *Planetary Energies: Mercury, Moon. Elemental Energies: Air, Water. Astrological Sign: Cancer.*

WILD CHERRY *(Prunus serotina).* Under the auspices of Venus, cherry bark has a sweet, woodsy aroma popular in many love spells and rituals. Combine with rose petals and cinnamon, then add a few drops of love oil for a great bedroom sachet. Mix with cedar, orange peel, and orris root for divination potpourri and a drop of divination oil for a great sachet. As cedar, cherry, and orange peel normally have exotic scents of their own, the orris root helps to hold the combined essence, which is especially handy for an on-the-go reader. If you want to sweeten a deal or attract a specific energy, cherry is an excellent addition to your spellwork. You might also consider adding bee pollen, sugar, and bergamot to a gris-gris bag that includes a magnet or lodestone and your desire written on parchment for financial endeavors, especially if you are dealing with the opposite sex who may be in opposition to your wishes. Cherry bark can also be included in all manner of beauty spells. *Planetary Energy: Venus. Elemental Energies: Air, Earth. Astrological Signs: Libra, Taurus.*

one
two
three
four
five

219

WINTERGREEN *(Gaultheria procumbens)*. Popular in gum, candy, and medicinals for muscle aches and pains, wintergreen was used by the Sioux Indians as a poultice and in colonial times as a replacement for tea; however, most of the wintergreen flavorings in food these days is synthetic, as wintergreen essential oil is considered highly toxic by the FDA if taken internally. Mix wintergreen, lavender, and mint in spells that focus on the protection of children. Combine with eucalyptus, rosemary, and hyssop for healing poppets and sachets. Throw wintergreen into the needfire, cauldron, or fire-festival bonfire for good luck during the current seasonal cycle. Some practitioners add wintergreen to spells involving astral travel, divination, and animal magick. *Planetary Energy: Mercury. Elemental Energies: Air, Earth. Astrological Signs: Gemini, Virgo.*

WITCH HAZEL *(Hamamelis virginiana)*. The witch hazel is a deciduous shrub with twisting stems; long, forking branches; and smooth grey to brownish bark. Growing well in misty woods, this hardy bush immediately leads the mind to enchantment and magick! Primarily used in spells for divination, clarity, and wisdom, witch hazel can also be employed when working healing magick to combat mental illness and low self-esteem. Used in crossing rituals (Wiccan funerals) to assist in combating the grief felt by the participants in the ceremony. The name "witch hazel" comes from an Old English word meaning "pliant" or "to bend." The limber branches of this plant were used as archery bows, and we can see how the association to magickal workers may have occurred—a Witch (in today's terms) learns to manifest from the primordial void by "bending" light, so to speak. *Planetary Energy: Saturn. Elemental Energy: Earth. Astrological Signs: Capricorn, Aquarius (classical).*

one
two
three
four
five

220

WOOD BETONY *(Stachys officinalis).* A protective herb often added to gris-gris bags or burned in combination with angelica, elecampane, horehound, or hyssop. Use in any ritual for a soldier, police officer, firefighter, or paramedic. Combine with safflower for victory and successful finance ventures; use with a red candle. *Planetary Energy: Mars. Elemental Energy: Fire. Astrological Sign: Aries.*

WOODRUFF *(Asperula odorata).* Also known as Master of the Woods. Used in magick for strength, protection, and the absence of pain. Combine with sunflower petals, St. John's wort, mugwort, and blessed thistle in a poppet for victory over obstacles of any kind. For money spells, add white beans and cinnamon and place in an open jar with a lodestone or crystal to draw money into the home or business. Dress with a money oil. *Planetary Energy: Mars. Elemental Energy: Fire. Astrological Sign: Aries.*

WORMWOOD *(Artemisia absinthium).* A major favorite in Hoodoo magick, wormwood is used to speak to the dead and call the spirits. In such southern magick it is used to work on an individual's conscience if they have done you wrong, or if they lie straight out in a court case or other venue where your reputation is at stake—however, if you are dealing with a psychopath that doesn't have a conscience, sending an astral dead guy might be a better idea. The formula for such conjuration includes myrrh, patchouli, clove, yerba maté, mullein, peppermint, lemon peel, and graveyard dirt. Spray mixture lightly with white rum. Note: Do not ingest this formula. On the brighter side, the herb can also be used as an increasing agent in success spells, especially if you are trying to increase your

one

two

three

four

five

221

current paycheck. Add to lobelia (gag root), plantain, and slippery elm to stop gossip. This is another one of those herbs considered by the FDA to be unhealthy for human consumption. *Planetary Energy: Mars. Elemental Energy: Fire. Astrological Sign: Aries.*

YARROW FLOWERS *(Achillea millefolium).* Yarrow was one of the first herbs I learned to work with both in a magickal and medicinal arena. Yarrow tea (which can be purchased at an herbal store) is wonderful for respiratory infections, especially if you are prone to bronchitis. However, at the same time I had a nasty cold I also had a doozy of a neighbor. The formula of yarrow, nettles, and hot peppers got that nasty neighbor gone in no time at all. A little sprinkled on the doorstep will do ya. Primarily used for its exorcism properties, yarrow mixed with hawthorn, trillium, linden, gotu kola ("life everlasting"), and dried rosebuds can be used in a handfasting/marriage sachet to be carried in the bridal bouquet, then placed under the bridal bed to ensure a long and happy marriage. One of those all-purpose herbs, yarrow can be used in animal magick, divination, to increase the power of a spell, for breaking spells, and in fertility rituals. *Planetary Energy: Moon. Elemental Energy: Water. Astrological Sign: Cancer.*

YELLOW DOCK ROOT *(Rumex crispus).* With Jupiter as its ruling planet, this herb's primary function is one of expansion. The leaves of the yellow dock are spiky and the seeds look like little hearts, thus it contains the idea of protecting the heart of the matter and expanding the central focal point of an issue. In magick, yellow dock is said to remove the bad blood from a financial situation and make way for growth and monetary success. A prime ingredient to bring money into a business, yellow dock should be brought over the front threshold of the establishment and placed in a bowl of water along with a lodestone or magnet to attract solid, paying customers, with the light of a yellow candle reflecting off the surface of the bowl. If you are running low on fast cash, sprinkle a bit of yellow dock on your remaining funds (you know, those quarters you found under the couch cushions). The herb has other magickal uses, including marriage (with yarrow) in fertility spells. If it sets for long periods of time, yellow dock will stain white cloth. This can be useful! Wrap yellow dock and white cotton gris-gris bags in a plastic bag and allow to age. Bags will pick up the color and vibrations of the plant. Use them later on in the year for prosperity spells. For a "root of prosperity" formula designed to assist you to build a stable financial base, mix allspice, snakeroot, sarsaparilla, galangal, ginger, frankincense, yellow dock, fava beans, and tonka beans. Place mixture on a white plate. Burn a white or golden candle (in a fire-safe holder) in the center of the mixture. *Planetary Energy: Jupiter. Elemental Energies: Fire, Water. Astrological Signs: Sagittarius, Pisces (classical).*

one
two
three
four
five

223

YERBA MATÉ *(Ilex paraguensis).* A Hoodoo favorite, a little over two years ago I went nuts looking for this herb in my area. I finally found it in tea form at a health-food store and had to make do with that until I could find a supplier that could mail it to me. This is the number-one additive in any spell to banish nightmares, make problems disappear, and diminish worries, pain, sorrow, or discomfort. Add to any exorcism or purification mixture for that added punch. Also used in dieting spells or spells in which you wish to diminish an issue on which you have been so focused that you have ignored all other things and now your world is out of balance. *Planetary Energy: Saturn. Elemental Energies: Earth, Air. Astrological Signs: Capricorn, Aquarius (classical).*

one

two

three

four

five

✦

224

YERBA SANTA *(Eriodictyon sp.).* Sometimes called the holy or sacred herb, yerba santa is a primary ingredient in glamouries and spells of illusion. Include in healing work by combining with heal-all, lavender, and eucalyptus. Sometimes worn to increase clarity, used in divinatory herbal mixes and gris-gris bags for spiritual strength. *Elemental Energy: Earth. Planetary Energy: Venus. Astrological Sign: Taurus.*

YOHIMBE POWDER *(Corynanthe yohimbe).* The equivalent to dragon's blood, yohimbe is also expensive, messy, and powerful. In fact, it is difficult to tell the two herbs apart; however, yohimbe is more on the brown side. This is another herb that is not recommended for human consumption by the FDA and therefore is only used in magickal applications. As it is a powder, care should be taken when working with this particular herb not to inhale the particles. Yohimbe is used in spellwork to Command (with a big "c"). It is an authoritative herb, one that demands that the work be done. Use in combination with patchouli and other power herbs if you need to produce magick with gusto. This is a vibrant, forceful herb used to break blocks, destroy obstacles, and add more bounce to the ounce in matters of the heart. *Planetary Energy: Venus. Elemental Energy: Earth. Astrological Sign: Taurus.*

The herbal information provided in this section took me three years to compile and is representative of my own experiences in working hundreds of spells and rituals for a variety of situations, some practical and others very strange indeed. The life of a Witch is certainly never boring!

Summary

As I close yet another visit with you, my youngest son is entering his last year of high school and about the month the book is released he will be graduating. Echo is in college and working full time. Falcon is three-quarters through a tour in the army as a medic and has just returned from overseas. My oldest son is leaving for an overseas tour in the military service. This past summer, my three adult children took their oath of third degree in the world of Witchcraft. Through the years, fans all over the world have visited with my family, had a few laughs and witnessed a few tears . . . I bet some of you can even remember when my kids were small! It was a pleasure and a joy as I and other Black Forest members welcomed these three into the "big Witches" circle. Their journey, once again, has just begun—this time into the world of Craft adulthood.

This is definitely a year of closure for me with many bright avenues ahead. I wish you the same success and joy I have experienced in developing this material—but without any of the pitfalls that daily life can throw at you! I will finish out by writing the same words given to my daughter with each missive when she spent that perilous time overseas.

Be safe.

Keep smiling.

And may the Lord and Lady be with you.

IS (In Service),

Silver RavenWolf

one

two

three

four

five

225

References

Blumenthal, Mark. *The ABC Clinical Guide to Herbs.* Thieme
Medical Publishers: New York, New York. 2003.

Botanical Safety Handbook. Edited by Michael McGuffin,
Christopher Hobbs, Roy Upton, and Alicia Goldberg.
CRC Press: Boca Raton, Florida. 1997.

Cunningham, Scott. *Cunningham's Encyclopedia of Magical
Herbs.* Llewellyn Publications: St. Paul, Minnesota. 1988.

Eastman, John. *The Book of Field and Roadside: Open Country
Weeds, Trees, and Wildflowers of Eastern North America.* Stack-
pole Books: Mechanicsburg, Pennsylvania. 2003.

Foster, Steven, and James A. Duke. *Eastern/Central Medicinal
Plants: Peterson Field Guides.* Houghton Mifflin Company:
Boston, Massachusetts. 1990.

Hall, Judy. *The Illustrated Guide to Crystals.* Sterling Publishing
Company: New York, New York. 2000.

Kowalchik, Claire, and Hylton Kowalchik. *William H. Rodale's
Illustrated Encyclopedia of Herbs.* Rodale Press, Inc.: Em-
maus, Pennsylvania. 1998.

*Life Extension, Disease Prevention and Treatment: Scientific
Protocols that Integrate Mainstream and Alternative Medicine.*
Expanded Third Edition. Melanie Segala, editor. The Life
Extension Foundation: Hollywood, Florida. 2000.

Muller-Ebeling, Claudia, Christian Ratsch, and Wolf-Dieter Storl. *Witchcraft Medicine: Healing Arts, Shamanic Practices, and Forbidden Plants.* Inner Traditions: Rochester, Vermont. 2003.

Nierring, William, Nancy Olmstead, and John Thieret. *National Audubon Society Field Guide to North American Wildflowers Eastern Region.* Alfred A. Knopf: New York, New York. 2001.

PDR for Herbal Medicines. Third edition. Thomson Healthcare, Inc.: Montvale, New Jersey. ND.

The Plant Book: An Encyclopedia of Worldwide Flora. James Mills-Hicks, publisher. Random House: Australia. 2001.

Smith, Steven. *Wylundt's Book of Incense.* Samuel Weiser, Inc.: York Beach, Maine. 1966.

Talbot, Rob, and Robin Whiteman. *Brother Cadfael's Herb Garden: An Illustrated Companion to Medieval Plants and Their Uses.* Little, Brown and Company: London, England. 1996.

Wood, Matthew. *The Book of Herbal Wisdom: Using Plants As Medicines.* North Atlantic Books: Berkeley, California. 1997.

Yronwode, Catherine. *Hoodoo Herb and Root Magic.* Lucky Mojo Curio Company: Forestville, California. 2002.

Appendices

I: Color Magick Correspondences

Use the lists below when in doubt, but don't view this information as the last word on color magick.

COLOR	PURPOSE
Black	Returning to sender; divination; negative work; protection
Blue–Black	For wounded pride; broken bones; angelic protection
Dark Purple	Used for calling up the power of the ancient ones; sigils/runes; government
Lavender	To invoke righteous spirit within yourself and favors for people
Dark Green	Invoking the goddess of regeneration; agriculture; financial
Mint Green	Financial gains (used with gold and silver)
Green	Healing or health; north cardinal point
Avocado Green	Beginnings
Light Green	Improve the weather
Indigo Blue	To reveal deep secrets; protection on the astral levels; defenses
Dark Blue	To create confusion (must be used with white or you will confuse yourself)
Blue	Protection
Royal Blue	Power and protection
Pale/Light Blue	Protection of home; buildings; young; young males
Ruby Red	Love or anger of a passionate nature
Red	Love; romantic atmosphere; energy; south cardinal point

COLOR	PURPOSE
Light Red	Deep affection of a nonsexual nature
Deep Pink	Harmony and friendship in the home
Pink	Harmony and friendship with people; binding magick
Pale Pink	Friendship; young females
Yellow	Healing; can also represent east cardinal point
Deep Gold	Prosperity; sun magick
Gold	Attraction
Pale Gold	Prosperity in health
Burnt Orange	Opportunity
Orange	Material gain; to seal a spell; attraction
Dark Brown	Invoking earth for benefits
Brown	Peace in the home; herb magick; friendship
Pale Brown	Material benefits in the home
Silver	Quick money; gambling; invocation of the moon; moon magick
Off-White	Peace of mind
Lily White	Mother candle (burned for thirty minutes at each moon phase)
White	Righteousness; purity; used for east cardinal point; devotional magick
Gray	Glamouries

230

Use white to substitute for any color.

Colors for Days of the Week

Monday	White
Tuesday	Red
Wednesday	Purple
Thursday	Green
Friday	Blue
Saturday	Black
Sunday	Yellow

II: Planetary Hours[1]

The selection of an auspicious time for beginning a magickal working is an important matter. When a thing is begun, its existence takes on the nature of the conditions under which it was begun. Each hour of the day is ruled by a planet and takes on the attributes of that planet. You will notice that planetary hours do not take into account Uranus, Neptune, and Pluto, as they are considered here as higher octaves of Mercury, Venus, and Mars, respectively. For example, if something is ruled by Uranus, you can use the hour of Mercury. The only other factor you need to know to use the planetary hours is the time of your local sunrise and sunset for any given day, available from your local newspaper. *Note:* Your sunrise and sunset time may vary from the example if you live in a different location. Your latitude/longitude are already figured into your local paper's sunrise and sunset times.

> STEP ONE. From your local paper, find the sunrise and sunset times for your location and your chosen day. We will use January 2, 1999, 10 degrees latitude, as an example. Sunrise for January 2, 1999, at 10 degrees latitude is at 6 hours and 16 minutes (or 6:16 AM) and sunset is at 17 hours and 49 minutes (or 5:49 PM).

> STEP TWO. Subtract sunrise time (6 hours 16 minutes) from sunset time (17 hours 49 minutes) to get the number of astrological daylight hours. It is easier to do this if you convert the hours into minutes. For example, 6 hours and 16 minutes equals 376 minutes. 17 hours and 49 minutes equals 1,069 minutes. Now subtract: 1,069 minutes minus 376 minutes equals 693 minutes.

---

1. Planetary hour information is condensed from Llewellyn's 2000 Daily Planetary Guide, pp. 184–185.

STEP THREE. Next you should determine how many minutes are in a daylight planetary hour for that particular day. To do this, divide 693 minutes (the number of daylight minutes) by 12. The answer is 58, rounded off. Therefore, a daylight planetary hour for January 2, 1999, at 10 degrees latitude has 58 minutes.

STEP FOUR. Now you know that each daylight planetary hour is roughly 58 minutes. You also know, from step one, that sunrise is at 6:16 AM. To determine the starting times of each planetary hour, simply add 58 minutes to the sunrise time for the first planetary hour, 58 minutes to that number for the second planetary hour, etc. Therefore, the first hour in our example is 6:16 AM–7:14 AM. The second hour is 7:14 AM–8:12 AM, and so on. Note that because you rounded up the number of minutes in a sunrise hour, the last hour doesn't end exactly at sunset. This is a good reason to give yourself a little "fudge space" when using planetary hours. (You could also skip the rounding-up step.)

STEP FIVE. Now, to determine which sign rules which daylight planetary hour, consult your calendar to determine which day of the week January 2 falls on. You'll find it's a Saturday in 1999. Next, turn to page 233 to find the sunrise planetary hour chart. If you follow down the column for Saturday, you will see that the first hour is ruled by Saturn, the second by Jupiter, the third by Mars, and so on.

STEP SIX. Now you've determined the daytime (sunrise) planetary hours. You can use the same formula to determine the nighttime (sunset) planetary hours, using sunset as your beginning time and sunrise the next day as your end time. When you get to step 5, remember to consult the sunset table on page 234 rather than the sunrise table.

PLANETARY HOURS
SUNRISE

Hour	Sunday	Monday	Tuesday	Wednesday	Thursday	Friday	Saturday
1	Sun	Moon	Mars	Mercury	Jupiter	Venus	Saturn
2	Venus	Saturn	Sun	Moon	Mars	Mercury	Jupiter
3	Mercury	Jupiter	Venus	Saturn	Sun	Moon	Mars
4	Moon	Mars	Mercury	Jupiter	Venus	Saturn	Sun
5	Saturn	Sun	Moon	Mars	Mercury	Jupiter	Venus
6	Jupiter	Venus	Saturn	Sun	Moon	Mars	Mercury
7	Mars	Mercury	Jupiter	Venus	Saturn	Sun	Moon
8	Sun	Moon	Mars	Mercury	Jupiter	Venus	Saturn
9	Venus	Saturn	Sun	Moon	Mars	Mercury	Jupiter
10	Mercury	Jupiter	Venus	Saturn	Sun	Moon	Mars
11	Moon	Mars	Mercury	Jupiter	Venus	Saturn	Sun
12	Saturn	Sun	Moon	Mars	Mercury	Jupiter	Venus

233

PLANETARY HOURS
SUNSET

Hour	Sunday	Monday	Tuesday	Wednesday	Thursday	Friday	Saturday
1	Jupiter	Venus	Saturn	Sun	Moon	Mars	Mercury
2	Mars	Mercury	Jupiter	Venus	Saturn	Sun	Moon
3	Sun	Moon	Mars	Mercury	Jupiter	Venus	Saturn
4	Venus	Saturn	Sun	Moon	Mars	Mercury	Jupiter
5	Mercury	Jupiter	Venus	Saturn	Sun	Moon	Mars
6	Moon	Mars	Mercury	Jupiter	Venus	Saturn	Sun
7	Saturn	Sun	Moon	Mars	Mercury	Jupiter	Venus
8	Jupiter	Venus	Saturn	Sun	Moon	Mars	Mercury
9	Mars	Mercury	Jupiter	Venus	Saturn	Sun	Moon
10	Sun	Moon	Mars	Mercury	Jupiter	Venus	Saturn
11	Venus	Saturn	Sun	Moon	Mars	Mercury	Jupiter
12	Mercury	Jupiter	Venus	Saturn	Sun	Moon	Mars

III: Moon Phases

NEW MOON

- Moon is 0–45 degrees directly ahead of the Sun
- Moon rises at dawn, sets at sunset; for full use of these energies, stick between this time period
- Moon is from exact New Moon to 3½ days after
- Purpose: Beginnings
- Workings: Beauty, health, self-improvement, farms and gardens, job hunting, love and romance, networking, creative ventures
- Pagan Holiday: Winter Solstice (December 22)[2]
- Goddess Name: Rosemerta's Moon
- Goddess Energy: Goddesses of Growth
- Offering: Milk and honey
- Theme: Abundance
- Rune: Feoh for abundance; Cen for openings; Gyfu for love
- Tarot Trump: The Fool

CRESCENT

- Moon is 45–90 degrees ahead of the Sun
- Moon rises at midmorning, sets after sunset; for full use of these energies, stick between this time period
- Moon is from 3½ to 7 days after the New Moon
- Purpose: The movement of the thing
- Workings: Animals, business, change, emotions, matriarchal strength

---

2. Due to astrological timing, solstices and equinoxes will not always be on the same date. Other Pagan holidays will differ depending on the tradition practiced.

- Pagan Holiday: Imbolc (February 1)
- Goddess Name: Brigid's Moon
- Goddess Energy: Water Goddesses
- Offering: Candles
- Theme: Manifestation
- Rune: Birca for beginnings; Ing for focus
- Tarot Trump: The Magician

FIRST QUARTER

- Moon is 90–135 degrees ahead of the Sun
- Moon rises at noon, sets at midnight; for full use of these energies, stick between this time period
- Moon is from 7 to 10½ days after the New Moon
- Purpose: The shape of the thing
- Workings: Courage, elemental magick, friends, luck, and motivation
- Pagan Holiday: Spring Equinox (March 21)
- Goddess Name: Persephone's Moon
- Goddess Energy: Air Goddesses
- Offering: Feathers
- Theme: Luck
- Rune: Algiz for luck; Jera for improvement; Ur for strength
- Tarot Card: Strength or The Star

GIBBOUS

- Moon is 135–180 degrees ahead of the Sun
- Moon rises in midafternoon, sets around 3 AM; for full use of these energies, stick between this time period
- Moon is between 10½ to 14 days after the New Moon

- Purpose: Details
- Workings: Courage, patience, peace, harmony
- Pagan Holiday: Beltaine (May 1)
- Goddess Name: Nuit's Moon
- Goddess Energy: Star Goddesses
- Offering: Ribbons
- Theme: Perfection
- Rune: Asa for eloquence; Wyn for success; Dag for enlightenment
- Tarot Trump: The World

FULL MOON

- Moon is 180–225 degrees ahead of the Sun
- Moon rises at sunset, sets at dawn; for full use of these energies, stick between this time period
- Moon is from 14 to 17½ days after the New Moon
- Purpose: Completion of a project
- Workings: Artistic endeavors, beauty, health, fitness, change, decisions, children, competition, dreams, families, health, knowledge, legal undertakings, love, romance, money, motivation, protection, psychic power, self-improvement
- Pagan Holiday: Summer Solstice (June 21)
- Goddess Name: Sekhmet's Moon
- Goddess Energy: Fire Goddesses
- Offering: Flowers
- Theme: Power
- Rune: Sol
- Tarot Card: The Sun

DISSEMINATING

- Moon is 225–270 degrees ahead of the Sun
- Moon rises at midevening, sets at midmorning; for full use of these energies, stick between this time frame
- Moon is 3½ to 7 days after the Moon
- Purpose: Initial destruction
- Workings: Addiction, decisions, divorce, emotions, stress, protection
- Pagan Holiday: Lammas (August 1)
- Goddess Name: Hecate's Moon
- Goddess Energy: Earth Goddesses
- Offering: Grain or rice
- Theme: Reassessment
- Rune: Thorn for destruction; Algiz for protection; Thorn for defense
- Tarot Trump: The Tower for destruction; Hope for protection

238

LAST QUARTER

- Moon is 270–315 degrees ahead of the Sun
- Moon rises at midnight and sets at noon; for full use of these energies, stick between this time frame
- Moon is 7 to 10½ days after the Full Moon
- Purpose: Absolute destruction
- Workings: Addictions, divorce, endings, health and healing (banishing), stress, protection, ancestors
- Pagan Holiday: Fall Equinox (September 21)
- Goddess Name: The Morrigan's Moon
- Goddess Energy: Harvest Goddesses

- Offering: Incense
- Theme: Banishing
- Rune: Hagal; Ken for banishing; Nyd for turning; Isa for binding
- Tarot Trump: Judgement

BALSAMIC (DARK MOON)

- Moon is 315–360 degrees ahead of the Sun
- Moon rises at 3 AM, sets midafternoon; for full use of these energies, stick between this time frame
- Moon is 10½ to 14 days after the Full Moon
- Purpose: Rest
- Workings: Addictions, change, divorce, enemies, justice, obstacles, quarrels, removal, separation, stopping stalkers and theft
- Pagan Holiday: Samhain (October 31)
- Goddess Name: Kali's Moon
- Goddess Energy: Dark Goddesses
- Offering: Honesty
- Theme: Justice
- Rune: Tyr for justice; Ken for banishing
- Tarot Trump: Justice

Index

Free Magazine

Read unique articles by Llewellyn authors, recommendations by experts, and information on new releases. To receive a **free** copy of Llewellyn's consumer magazine, *New Worlds of Mind & Spirit,* simply call 1-877-NEW-WRLD or visit our website at www.llewellyn.com and click on *New Worlds.*

LLEWELLYN ORDERING INFORMATION

Order Online:
Visit our website at www.llewellyn.com, select your books, and order them on our secure server.

Order by Phone:
- Call toll-free within the U.S. at 1-877-NEW-WRLD (1-877-639-9753). Call toll-free within Canada at 1-866-NEW-WRLD (1-866-639-9753)
- We accept VISA, MasterCard, and American Express

Order by Mail:
Send the full price of your order (MN residents add 7% sales tax) in U.S. funds, plus postage & handling to:

Llewellyn Worldwide
P.O. Box 64383, Dept. 0-7387-0662-0
St. Paul, MN 55164-0383, U.S.A.

Postage & Handling:

Standard (U.S., Mexico, & Canada). If your order is:
$49.99 and under, add $3.00
$50.00 and over, FREE STANDARD SHIPPING

AK, HI, PR: $15.00 for one book plus $1.00 for each additional book.

International Orders (airmail only):
$16.00 for one book plus $3.00 for each additional book

Orders are processed within 2 business days.
Please allow for normal shipping time. Postage and handling rates subject to change.

Solitary Witch

*The Ultimate Book of Shadows
for the New Generation*

Silver RavenWolf

The BIG book for Pagan teens

This book has everything a teen Witch could want and need between two covers: a magickal cookbook, encyclopedia, dictionary, and grimoire. It relates specifically to today's young adults and their concerns, yet is grounded in the magickal work of centuries past.

Information is arranged alphabetically and divided into five distinct categories: (1) Shadows of Religion and Mystery, (2) Shadows of Objects, (3) Shadows of Expertise and Proficiency, (4) Shadows of Magick and Enchantment, and (5) Shadows of Daily Life. It is organized so readers can skip over the parts they already know, or read each section in alphabetical order.

0-7387-0319-2

8 x 10, 608 pp., 53 illus., appendices, index $19.95

To order, call 1-877-NEW-WRLD

Prices subject to change without notice

Silver's Spells for Protection
Silver RavenWolf

Take the word "victim" out of your vocabulary

What do you do when you discover that your best friend at work sabotaged your promotion? Or if a neighbor suddenly decides that you don't belong in his town? What if a group of teens sets out to make your life a living hell? *Silver's Spells for Protection* contains tips for dealing with all these situations, and more.

This book covers how to handle stalkers, abusers, and other nasties with practical information as well as magickal techniques. It also discusses some of the other irritants in life—like protecting yourself from your mother-in-law's caustic tongue and how to avoid that guy who's out to take your job.

1-56718-729-3
208 pp., 5³⁄₁₆ x 8

$9.95

Silver's Spells for Abundance
Silver RavenWolf

Your Prosperity Spellbook

Tired of living paycheck to paycheck? Wish you could afford your dream home? Want better luck with investments? There's nothing like a little magick for bringing abundance into your life.

This gem of a spellbook is packed full of magickal workings to help you create abundance, get out of debt, and make money a positive force in your life. *Silver's Spells for Abundance* will show you how to:

- Prepare incenses, oils, and powders for prosperity
- Manifest desires through the Golden Cord
- Invite wealth into your home with a Prosperity Gourd
- Banish debt by constructing a Magic Bill Box
- Invoke the elements for financial assistance

. . . and learn dozens of spells for bringing bounty to your bank account!

0-7387-0525-X
192 pp., 5³⁄₁₆ x 8 $9.95

To order, call 1-877-NEW-WRLD
Prices subject to change without notice

To Write to the Author

If you wish to contact the author or would like more information about this book, please write to the author in care of Llewellyn Worldwide and we will forward your request. Both the author and publisher appreciate hearing from you and learning of your enjoyment of this book and how it has helped you. Llewellyn Worldwide cannot guarantee that every letter written to the author can be answered, but all will be forwarded. Please write to:

Silver RavenWolf
⁒ Llewellyn Worldwide
P.O. Box 64383, Dept. 0-7387-0662-0
St. Paul, MN 55164-0383, U.S.A.

Please enclose a self-addressed stamped envelope for reply,
or $1.00 to cover costs. If outside U.S.A., enclose
international postal reply coupon.

Many of Llewellyn's authors have websites with additional information and resources. For more information, please visit our website:

HTTP://WWW.LLEWELLYN.COM